Active Learning

in the Middle Grades Classroom

Susan Edwards

Association for Middle Level Education

Printed in the United States of America.

ISBN 978-1-56090-285-0

Library of Congress Cataloging-in-Publication Date

Names: Edwards, Susan, 1975- author.
Title: Active learning in the middle grades classroom / Susan Edwards.
Description: Westerville : Associaton for Middle Level Education, [2016] |
    Includes bibliographical references.
Identifiers: LCCN 2016036485 (print) | LCCN 2016039014 (ebook) | ISBN
    9781560902850 (pbk.) | ISBN 9781560902867 (electronic PDF)
Subjects: LCSH: Middle school teaching--United States. | Active
    learning--United States.
Classification: LCC LB1623.5 .E39 2016 (print) | LCC LB1623.5 (ebook) |
DDC
    373.1102--dc23
LC record available at https://lccn.loc.gov/2016036485

Association for Middle Level Education
4151 Executive Parkway, Suite 300
Westerville, Ohio 43081 | amle.org

Dedication

To all of the middle school teachers who are brave enough to teach in the way that their students learn best.

Acknowledgements

I would like to thank my husband, Steve, for his patience and continual support. He never seems to tire of cheering me on.

Thanks to the teachers in my research study who willingly allowed me into their classrooms so that I could learn from them. And I did.

A special thanks to Tanya McLain who is the energizer bunny of active learning. It is so refreshing to see so much energy and determination put into doing what is best for students.

Thanks to Judi Wilson and Beth Pendergraft who are so generous with their time and advice. Thank you for always being willing to help me "think through something".

Thanks to Jennifer Armstrong who constantly provided ideas, resources, and encouragement.

I would also like to thank all of the educators that I have gotten ideas from over the years. I have learned so many things from so many middle school educators and I know that their voices are underneath the ideas in this book. I cited them where I could, but I do not always have a record of the origin of every idea I have gotten from someone else.

Biography

Dr. Susan Edwards is an associate professor at Augusta University in Augusta, Georgia, where she teaches middle grades education and math education courses. With more than 25 years of experience in the field of middle grades education, Edwards focuses her scholarly research on active learning in the middle grades classroom.

Table of Contents

Part 1
Active Learning Framework

Part 2
Practical Classroom Strategies

Part 3
What Active Learning Looks Like in the Classroom

Part 4:
Overcoming Barriers

Introduction

The Voices of Students

I have had the wonderful opportunity to talk about teaching and learning with the different stakeholders in education as I spent my career in a middle school classroom, a school district office, and a university setting. I noticed that academics often talk to other academics about theory and research, teachers talk to other teachers about the daily struggles of teaching, and students talk to other students about what is boring and what is interesting in the classroom. This book incorporates all of those voices—different groups of people valuing middle grades education from different perspectives. There are the voices of academics who have spent much time examining theory and doing research to help discover effective teaching approaches. There are the voices of the many excellent teachers implementing effective teaching strategies every day in middle school classrooms across America. And finally, there are the voices of middle grades students who have much to say about what they do and do not like and how they learn best.

Because, ultimately, it is middle grades students we are trying to engage, we begin by listening to their voices first as I share information gleaned from my interviews of seventh graders about the types of instructional activities they enjoy and what helps them learn. These are not fictitious students or children of rocket scientists, but typical young adolescents. As such, it will not surprise you to learn that they had many opinions, and they were not afraid to express those opinions.

On Worksheets...

It would be hard to imagine how many trees have been cut over the last 100 years so middle grades students can complete worksheets. Admittedly, all worksheets are not created equal. Some require students to be actively involved in their learning, while some just ask students to mindlessly recopy information from the notes they just copied from a PowerPoint. Although I do not advocate abolishing all worksheets, I do suggest that we do fewer. Middle grades students would celebrate such a change—they are tired of the worksheets.

> *I don't like worksheets, they don't help you learn; they are like a punishment.* (Xavier)

Not surprisingly the most common reason the students gave for not liking worksheets was that they were boring.

> *No, I do not like worksheets. I don't like worksheets because they are boring and they waste my time.* (Camila).

However, some students had insight into the value and purpose of completing worksheets. They were able to identify different types and purposes of worksheets.

I believe that worksheets are helpful to a certain extent because writing things helps me remember, but after a while, it becomes more about getting the right answer to get a good grade instead of knowing what you're writing about. (Shaniqua)

I don't like when we have to do those worksheets where you find the answers in the textbooks because most of the time we aren't really reading it; we are just looking for the answers. We write the answer down, and we don't think twice about what we are reading and just write the answer. (Ashley)

I don't like worksheets and I don't believe they help me learn. They help me remember. (Seung)

Although the students were not big fans of worksheets, they did have lots of ideas about active learning.

I want my teachers to do fun activities because I don't want to do boring activities all period. (Deon)

On Group Work...

I wish we would do more group work so that we could communicate and share our thoughts. (Ryan)

[I wish we could do more] partner work, so we can understand things from a different perspective. Also, we can take some things or methods that can help us with work from our partners. (Zoe)

I like group work because you don't have to stay quiet while you're working, and you can also ask if someone got a different answer. (Gabriela)

Yes, students understand it more when people of their own age help. (Keisha)

On Projects...

I wish our teachers would have us do more projects because I think projects are a chance to show teachers what you're made of. (Miya)

Projects are good, because you usually have to do a bit of research which you can learn from. (Nathan)

I like doing projects because when you look up information it could be something you never knew. (Emma)

Projects help you learn more about something you did not know before. Also it lets your teachers see if you are listening in class. (Lilly)

On Games...

I think games are a great way to learn because games are fun and enjoyable. I am more likely to pay attention to something I enjoy. (Antwan)

I wish teachers would have us play more games because it makes learning more fun and it helps me not zone out. (Lashonda)

I believe that we should be able to play more games in the classroom because it keeps us interactive. We don't know that we are learning—we are just learning. And it is making us have fun while the teacher is doing stuff. (Miguel)

On Presentations...

Yes I do think we should do presentations, I think it's fun for everybody to see how hard you worked to make something and then say it out loud in front of the classroom. (Luke)

I think presentations help us to learn and to become less nervous because you're getting used to speaking in front of people. (Aisha)

I like presentations because presentations get you used to talking in front of people. And like when you go to college, you aren't going to go through college and high school without doing presentations. So, if you know how to do it now, it's going to be easier in college, and that's when it actually matters a lot. (Dallas)

I agree with Matt's approach. He suggests a balanced approach to instruction that involves multiple learning approaches:

I think that both ways are good. Doing the activities and worksheets because on the worksheet you can visualize it but it is more fun to play with activities. I like both. Just put them together. (Matt)

Of course, learning is not just about having fun with the chance of gaining knowledge in the meantime. Learning is the top priority; if fun happens in addition, that is icing on the cake. Experts agree with these seventh graders on the importance of active learning. The first chapter discusses the many good reasons educational theorists give for active learning. After discussing the rationale for active learning in the middle grades classroom, the book introduces a framework for thinking about it. But the majority of the book is filled with practical strategies that make active learning doable in the classroom. Finally, the book concludes with a discussion of how to overcome the many obstacles and barriers that tend to get in the way of implementing active learning.

Part One

Introduction

The Active Learning Framework

The Association for Middle Level Education (AMLE) recommends that middle grades students be engaged in active, purposeful learning (National Middle School Association [NMSA], 2010). This section lays out a framework for active learning, but it is important to not lose the word **purposeful** in the discussion. The middle grades students you just heard from were interested in active learning mainly because it was "fun." As education professionals, we are only too aware that there is too much content to explore and too many thinking skills to develop just to have a good time. It is fine if fun happens as a by-product, but the goal is learning. The emphasis of active learning is the **purposeful** part. As the teacher, you need to be clear on the learning purpose for every instructional activity in your precious class time.

Three dimensions of active learning are important for young adolescents who learn best if they are intellectually, socially, and physically active as they are learning. Although they need not necessarily be engaged in all three of these dimensions at the same time each is important to their learning. Part One explores the Active Learning Framework shown below and explains the rationale for each of these dimensions that are critical to the successful learning of young adolescents.

Active Learning Framework

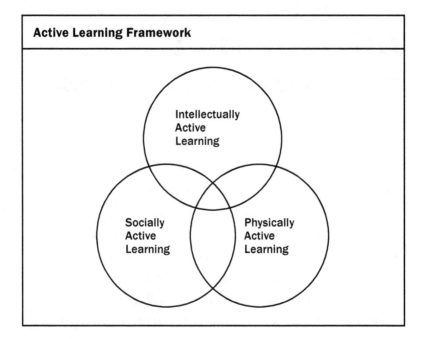

Chapter 1

What is Active Learning?

Teachers open the door; you enter by yourself.
~Chinese proverb

John Dewey describes learning as "something an individual does when he studies. It is an active, personally conducted affair" (1924, p. 390). There is a difference between learning facts and learning to do something with those facts. If we expect students to apply the knowledge they are learning in our classrooms, then we must help them develop the intellectual tools and problem-solving skills necessary to practice doing something with what they are learning (Michael, 2006). Students learn by becoming involved (Astin, 1985). When we involve students in learning activities that require them to discuss, question, clarify, and apply, they will retain the content we want them to remember better. Through active learning students are more likely to learn how to ask meaningful questions and become empowered to become lifelong learners.

This chapter begins by laying a foundation for teachers who are interested in using active learning. Active learning is defined and the theory behind it is discussed. Also discussed is what the research tells us about young adolescent development as a rationale for doing active learning with middle graders. Finally, the framework for thinking about active learning from three viewpoints—intellectual activity, social activity, and physical activity—will be explained.

Active Learning Defined

Active learning is a term that has been used often in educational literature, but not specifically defined. As educators we have almost taken a "you know it when you see it" approach to defining active learning. Consider the following range of classroom activities. At what point in the continuum shown in Figure 1 do the strategies become active learning strategies?

Figure 1: Active Learning Continuum

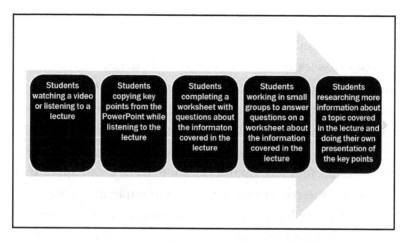

My answer would be… It depends. In this example, it depends mostly on the level of questions asked. Simply recalling or answering factual questions on the worksheet does not require much active learning. Students refer to their notes, whether or not they are working in small groups. But if students answer higher level questions that require them to compare and contrast different ideas or to argue different points of view, then active learning might occur further to the left.

The *Greenwood Dictionary of Education* defines active learning as:

> The process of having students engage in some activity that forces them to reflect upon ideas and how they are using those ideas. Requiring students to regularly assess their own degree of understanding and skill at handling concepts or problems in a particular discipline. The attainment of knowledge by participating or contributing. The process of keeping students mentally, and often physically, active in their learning through activities that involve them in gathering information, thinking, and problem solving. (Collins & O'Brien, 2003, p. 5)

Some key ideas fall within this definition. Student engagement is important and so is the idea of active participation. Students learn more if they are actively engaged in critical thinking and applying the content they are learning. Students must reflect on their own understanding and expand that understanding through a variety of means including discussions and explorations with classmates.

> We simply need to give students more time to dig beneath the surface, to grapple with the subject matter, and to make their own sense out of things. If we do, chances are they will be more likely to retain and use what we do give them. (Meyers & Jones, 1993, p. 14)

Bonwell and Eison (1991) offer some general characteristics of active learning in the classroom:

- Students are involved in more than listening.

- Less emphasis is placed on transmitting information and more on developing students' skills.

- Students are involved in higher-order thinking (analysis, synthesis, evaluation).

- Students are engaged in activities (e.g., reading, discussing, writing).

- Greater emphasis is placed on students' exploration of their own attitudes and values. (p. 1)

In other words, students must do more than listen, more than passively receive knowledge from either the teacher, a video, or the text, and they must do more than regurgitate pieces of information. Simply put, active learning means that students are "doing things and that they are thinking about what they are doing" (Bonwell & Eison, 1991, p. v).

Active vs. Passive Learning

One method of defining a term is to define what it is not. Often when educators think of the idea of active learning, they think of it in contrast to passive learning. Active learning conjures up an image of a classroom of excited students doing activities in small groups, while passive learning conjures up an image of rows of students facing the teacher who quietly and dutifully listen to her great wisdom. But rather than define active learning in terms of contrasting pictures in our minds, which could vary from person to person, we will identify three significant differences in the ideas of active learning and passive learning: (1) Active learning empowers the student to apply the knowledge that is learned, while passive learning imparts knowledge to the learner; (2) Active learning engages the student in higher-order thinking, while passive learning engages the student in factual learning; and (3) Active learning is student-centered, while passive learning is teacher-centered.

Empowering with Knowledge vs. Imparting Knowledge

Using a metaphor can sometimes help to describe a concept. There are various metaphors that people have used to describe passive learning that are rather appropriate and seem to be accurate descriptions of what is occurring between teachers and students in the passive learning approach. Passive learning is like downloading a PDF file from the Internet to your computer. You can download the file without reading it or thinking about it. You can dutifully save the file in a folder where you know you can retrieve it later if necessary and still not understand anything in the file. Richard Tiberius (1986) referred to passive learning pedagogy as "transmission" with the emphasis on "the efficient flow of information down the pipeline" (p. 148). In other words, teachers are viewed as effective if they can clearly, accurately, and efficiently transmit information to students. Paulo Freire (2001) talked about the "banking" concept of education. He believed that the way teacher and student relationships normally operated was similar to the teacher making deposits of information and students collecting those deposits, storing and cataloguing them, and retrieving them when necessary. But Friere felt that a much higher purpose should change this misguided system. He proposed:

For apart from inquiry, apart from the praxis, individuals cannot be truly human. Knowledge emerges only through invention and re-invention, through the restless, impatient continuing, hopeful inquiry human beings pursue in the world, with the world, and with each other. (p. 72)

Friere's ideas were along the lines of active learning. An active learning approach empowers learners, rather than making them passive recipients of deposits of information. In an active learning approach, students are empowered to uncover information on their own using a variety of resources, to grapple with new information until it makes sense, and to create new ideas using the information they have learned. Students also learn the tools that empower them to be lifelong learners who are capable of discovering and applying new ideas on their own, even when their schooling days are over and they no longer have the watchful guidance of a caring teacher to lead them.

Higher-Order Thinking vs. Factual Learning

With technology at our fingertips and unlimited pieces of information literally in the palms of our hands via smartphones, one could question the necessity of learning the thousands of facts that students memorize daily in our schools. Certainly there are facts and pieces of information every educated person should know, but it is not necessary to memorize as much as we do. Would it not be more productive to teach students how to retrieve factual information and apply it in new situations? Would it not be more important to teach students how to assess the validity and credibility of what they see on the Internet? Would it not be more important to teach students how to think critically and work collaboratively and creatively to solve unknown problems?

For example, when I was in fifth grade, I dutifully memorized the order of the planets from the sun. We practiced it in class many times. I believe there was some sort of mnemonic my teacher taught us to remember the order, but it escapes me now. I made a 100 on that test. All we had to do on the test was list the planets in order and of course, spell them correctly. I was a good memorizer and a good speller and my parents were happy with my A in science that quarter. Here is the rub though...if someone offered me a million dollars I could not list the planets in order, I am not even sure if I could list all nine (or is it eight now?). Maybe I could. I cannot say that I have ever needed to use that critical information I practiced so hard to remember in fifth grade. Should the need arise, thank goodness for Google. But I wonder whether I would have more interest now in astronomy or would have learned more about astronomy if my fifth grade teacher had involved me in active learning. I wonder whether I would have been more excited if someone had put a telescope in my hands or asked me some of the questions that perplexed the great astronomers in our history.

In an active learning approach, students do activities that require higher-order thinking. Students do things like solving problems and doing projects that require them to apply their new knowledge, synthesize new information, and analyze data to make generalizations. They grapple with questions that require critical thinking. In other words, they do something with the content information. In a passive learning approach, students focus on factual learning. The emphasis with a passive learning approach is memorization and recall of pieces of knowledge. This is not to say that students in active learning classrooms are not expected to learn factual information— they are. However, they learn those facts while in the process of doing something with them.

To illustrate this difference let's look into the classrooms of Mrs. Roberts and Mr. Williams. Mrs. Roberts is a firm believer in active learning while Mr. Williams is a firm believer in passive learning. Both of these teachers are teaching seventh grade mathematics and both are working on adding integers.

Active Learning Approach Mrs. Roberts' Classroom	Passive Learning Approach Mr. Williams' Classroom
Mrs. Roberts thinks it is important for students to have a conceptual understanding of what adding integers really means and therefore uses two hands-on activities to get across the concept. The students work with manipulatives called integer counters, and they also add problems on a giant number line in the classroom. Through doing multiple problems using both representations and looking at patterns in the problems and their answers, Mrs. Roberts leads her students into generalizing the rules for adding integers. She then gives them some word problems that require the addition of integers and lets the students figure them out together in small groups.	Mr. Williams thinks it is important for students to be able to efficiently and accurately add integers. He thinks that practice makes perfect and just like in sports, if the students add enough integer problems, they will be able to do it with automaticity. He presents the rules and spends a good deal of time making sure they are clear and every student can use them. He practices several problems with the class and then lets them practice many more similar problems on their own. When the students get stumped, he points to the rules on the board and he helps the students use the rules to find the answers.

Notice that the goals of the two teachers are different. Mrs. Roberts values conceptual understanding and application through problem solving. However, Mr. Williams values automaticity and using the rules accurately. Also notice that both teachers lead the students to the rules;

however, Mrs. Roberts has the students discover the rules for themselves, while Mr. Williams presents the rules to the students in the beginning.

Student-Centered vs. Teacher-Centered

Passive learning naturally occurs in a teacher-centered classroom, where students are expected to focus their attention on the teacher while he imparts knowledge to them. Active learning naturally occurs in a student-centered classroom, where students are the center of attention and often work together (but not always) as they are actively engaged in learning. Figure 2 shows the difference. In the teacher-centered classroom on the left (passive learning approach), the teacher is in the front of the room giving information and students are in desks facing him and quietly listening to his lecture. In the student-centered classroom on the right (active learning approach), the students are working together in small groups on a project. The teacher moves about the room and supports and guides students as they work on the project.

Figure 2: Teacher-Centered vs. Student-Centered Classroom

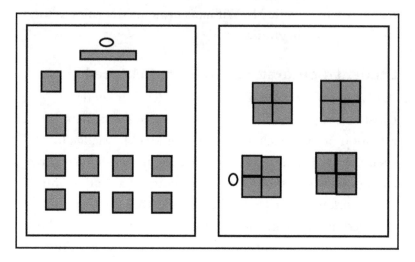

The roles of the teacher and students are very different in passive learning classrooms versus active learning classrooms. In a passive learning approach, the role of the teacher is to accurately and clearly impart knowledge. She may do this via lecture, demonstrations, working problems on the board, showing a video, or reading from a textbook. The role of students in a passive learning approach is to quietly listen and pay close attention. The students are to receive the information, store it in their memories, and retrieve it when necessary.

In an active learning approach, the role of the teacher is very different. The teacher plans, organizes, and choreographs purposeful activities that will lead the students to the desired understanding. The teacher serves as a facilitator, resource person, motivator, and guide (Petress, 2008). The teacher manages the learning environment to ensure that it is conducive to worthwhile learning. The role of the student in an active learning approach is to take a dynamic and energetic role in learning and through collaboration with peers and the teacher to actively seek out new knowledge and apply it to new contexts. Learning happens through combined efforts of students and the teacher. In both approaches the teacher is a source of discipline expertise, but in an active learning approach, the teacher is not considered the only source.

In an active learning classroom students work together collaboratively, while in a passive learning approach learning is mostly individual. An active learning classroom is a more hospitable place for a variety of student perspectives. Students are allowed and even encouraged to offer their own ideas and insights, offering justification for those ideas with evidence or facts that they have learned. During planning, teachers take student interests into account and often allow some choice. In a passive learning approach, the teacher's perspective is given preference and value.

An important theory that underlies the student-centered approach is humanism, which places focus on the learner. A humanistic approach relies on teacher-student relationships that are characterized by empathy, flexibility, authenticity, positive regard, and an understanding of the developmental and intellectual needs of the student. Students are seen as individuals who have unique backgrounds and needs (Cornelius-White & Harbaugh, 2010).

Active learning and passive learning are two different approaches to teaching content, but note that this is not necessarily an "all or nothing" dichotomy. It is possible for a teacher to engage students in an active learning approach on a Monday and then use a passive learning approach on a

Tuesday. However, there are many good reasons for favoring an active learning approach over a passive learning approach as Table 1 illustrates.

Table 1: Active Learning vs. Passive Learning

Active Learning	Passive Learning
Students are actively engaged in learning.	Students passively receive knowledge from the teacher.
Emphasis is on problem solving, application, and critical thinking.	Emphasis is on factual learning.
Collaborative learning is emphasized.	Individual learning is emphasized.
Students are the center of attention.	Teacher is the center of attention.
Teacher is a source of discipline expertise but also a facilitator of learning.	Teacher is the source of knowledge of the content.
Teacher designs, choreographs, and manages the learning environment.	Teacher is responsible for delivering content efficiently and accurately.
The classroom is a more hospitable place for a variety of student perspectives.	The teacher's perspective is given preference and value.
Students are empowered to seek out new knowledge and apply that knowledge in new contexts.	Students are viewed as empty vessels and a transmission approach is used to deliver knowledge.

Dewey and Active Learning

John Dewey was a philosopher and educational reformer often associated with the progressive movement in education.

Dewey was a champion of active learning. He emphasized the importance of experience in education and advocated for students to be involved in activities that engaged their hands and minds. Dewey shunned teaching that made students passive recipients of "bricks" of information (Dewey, 1924). Dewey also believed strongly in the idea of reflective activity. For Dewey, learning had not occurred until the student experienced a concept, reflected on that experience, and then took action based on that thinking (Narayan, Rodriguez, Araujo, Shaqlaih, & Moss, 2013). Because they are dependent on each other, thinking and action should not be separated, according to Dewey. He also thought it important for students to engage in activities that are as close to real life as possible and that the community of which they are a part should be represented in their learning experiences. Learning should be social and the learner should use what they have learned for social ends (Dewey, 1897). Dewey favored a project method in which students are intellectually active and overtly active in doing something with their learning, ideally something for the greater good of the community (Dewey, 1931).

Recommendations of the Association for Middle Level Education

The Association for Middle Level Education published a critical position paper in 2010, *This We Believe: Keys to Educating Young Adolescents*. In this publication, AMLE describes a framework containing four essential attributes and 16 characteristics of effective middle level schools. The 16 characteristics are further divided into three categories: (1) Curriculum, Instruction, and Assessment, (2) Leadership and Organization, and (3) Culture and Community (NMSA, 2010). One of the five Curriculum, Instruction, and Assessment principles recommends active learning: "Students and teachers are engaged in active, purposeful learning" (NMSA, 2010, p. 14).

Middle Schools Should Be Unique

Active learning is especially critical for young adolescents for a variety of reasons. First, young adolescents are at a unique place in their development (Nesin, 2012). They are at that in-between stage where they do not want to be treated like children and have moved on from the simple and very structured environment of their elementary school days. Yet, they are not quite young adults, and are not ready to assume the responsibilities of adulthood. Every middle grades teacher knows this transition well. At any given moment, middle grades students want to play games or go out for recess, while at the same time declaring that they do not want to be treated like babies and deserve freedom to do things on their own. Middle grades students really enjoy active learning strategies in the classroom. They enjoy a good academic game and often prefer this to sitting and listening to a "high-school-like" lecture. Although they want the freedom and privileges of high school students, they actually enjoy elementary school learning strategies.

We middle grades teachers can learn a lot from our elementary teacher colleagues. Of course, the traditional argument against using teaching methods similar to those used in elementary school instruction is that we need to prepare students for high school. But middle school is actually a time of transition. Rather than looking and feeling like an elementary or high school classroom, it should have the unique look and feel of a middle school classroom. As they use active learning throughout their middle school years, students should be guided to greater degrees of independence.

Variety

A second reason that active learning is ideal for middle grades students is that young adolescents crave variety. Frankly, they are tired of the worksheets. I do not know if anyone has done a research study that calculated the number of worksheets a typical student completes while in middle school, but my guess is the number would be disturbing. Students spend way too much time doing worksheets. We do not need to abolish worksheets from every middle school in the United States, but we should do fewer of them. Too many classrooms follow the same daily lesson plan. See if this sounds familiar:

> The students begin class with some sort of bell ringer activity, typically a practice test question. The teacher reviews the answers to last night's homework and gives the students an opportunity to ask questions. The teacher introduces the new concept for the day, usually with a PowerPoint. Students complete a worksheet practicing that concept. The teacher gives a homework assignment that might be questions from the textbook, a page in a workbook, or yet another worksheet.

Sound familiar? This standard lesson plan is repeated way too often, period after period, day after day, in the life of a typical middle grades student. In addition to the active learning principle, AMLE recommends multiple learning approaches (NMSA, 2010; Pate, 2013). Our classes are filled with a rich variety of students who come to our classrooms with different cultural experiences, different backgrounds, different preferences for learning, different interests, and so on. Our students are as unique as snowflakes. Using a variety of active learning strategies is respectful to the diversity of our students. You will find a higher level of engagement in students when every day is not like the day before. When you use a wide range of active learning strategies, more students have the opportunity to get engaged in the content. Structure is still important. Students need to expect regular procedures and routines in your classroom, but they learn more when doing a variety of learning activities from day to day. Brodhagen and Gorud (2012) assert that teachers are able to make a positive impact on student achievement if they implement multiple instructional approaches that recognize the wide diversity among middle grades students.

Value in the Struggle

A third reason that an active learning approach is ideal for young adolescents is that there is value in the struggle. We can all think of times in our lives when we had to work hard to learn something, but once we finally got it, we owned it. Our learning was not fragile or easily forgotten, because we struggled to obtain it in the first place. Harmin (1995) suggests that challenges enliven students and that young adolescents can handle more challenges. Using the term *challenge* in a positive way (not with the connotation of drudgery or a chore), he refers to it as "an exciting, adventurous, stretching opportunity, a chance to be brave and reach and conquer" (p.80). As adults we tend to want to shield young people from anything resembling discomfort, and we want to make their lives as easy as possible. Although the intent is kind, it is not a kind action in the end. Young adolescents need to be prepared to struggle to find answers and be able to handle the uncomfortable moment of confusion until they reach the breakthrough of understanding. Teachers need not purposely withhold information and put difficult roadblocks in front of students just to "toughen them up"—this only leads to students shutting down out of frustration. The teacher selects carefully designed activities that are within the reach of her students and scaffolds the activities at appropriate times while helping students secure the necessary resources to find out what they need to know.

Middle grades students are at an age when they are able to handle more and more independence in their learning carefully fostered by the teacher. As students progress through middle school, they need to gradually become more and more in charge of their own learning. Our goal should be to create autonomous learners who have the tools and skills necessary to be lifelong learners. Active learning requires that students develop the self-efficacy to believe that they can seek out new information and use that information to solve unknown problems in different contexts. Yes, our middle grades students need the nurturing guidance of a well-qualified teacher, but the outstanding teacher helps students believe that they are empowered to find it out on their own.

Active Learning Framework

Advocates for active learning in the middle grades agree that learning comes through direct experience and interaction with the intellectual, social, and physical environments (Edwards, Kemp, & Page, 2014; Nesin, 2012).

The active learning framework (see Figure 3) is a way of thinking about planning for active learning in the classroom. Of course, our first priority in the classroom is to get students intellectually active. We want them thinking at high levels, we want them problem solving, connecting ideas with other ideas, being creative, and engaging in critical thinking. We also want our students socially active in the classroom. We want them to work within the classroom community by doing projects together, collaborating, discussing, and working together to solve problems. But we also want them physically active. We want them doing things, using manipulatives, doing science experiences, role-playing, and creating models.

Certainly, you can be intellectually active at the same time you are socially active or physically active. A Venn diagram represents this framework because it is possible for an instructional method to fit in more than one dimension at the same time. For example, if students are asked to work in small groups to create a presentation on the lab experiment they just completed that required collecting data, analyzing data, and drawing conclusions, they would be engaged in intellectual, social, and physical active learning simultaneously. But it is also possible for an activity to fit into just one dimension, such as students individually creating a concept map of the chapter they just read. We will explore the ideas of intellectually active learning, socially active learning, and physically active learning in more depth in the next few sections.

Figure 3: Active Learning Framework

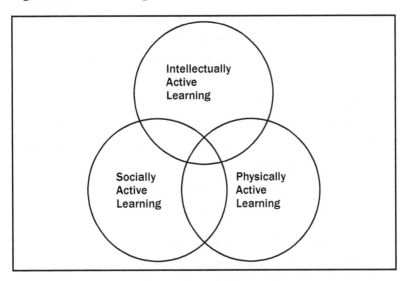

Intellectually Active Learning

Young adolescents are at a unique time in their intellectual development. They are at a place in their lives where they can begin thinking with more complexity. If teachers are aware of the typical characteristics of middle grades students, they can support their intellectual development using active learning strategies.

Concrete to Abstract

Piaget (1972) suggests four stages of cognitive development. The typical middle grades student is moving from the *Concrete Operational Stage to the Formal Operational Stage.* In Piaget's Concrete Operational Stage, which is typical for students 7–11 years of age, the student is able to think logically about ideas and events to which he or she has had direct exposure. When a young adolescent moves into Piaget's Formal Operational Stage, which is typical for students

11–15 years of age, the student can think more logically and abstractly, including things that are not within their direct realm of experience. Since middle grades students are moving from concrete to abstract thinking, active learning is ideal for helping students make this transition. Teachers can engage students in activities that include concrete representations, visual representations, and abstract or symbolic representations. By employing active learning, the teacher can move students strategically through these three representations, offering a bridge between the concrete and the abstract.

For example, if students are learning about protons, neutrons, and electrons in science, they could participate in a structured inquiry activity with balloons and paper to examine how they react to each other and to rubbing that creates a static charge. This would be a concrete representation of the phenomenon. Next, the teacher could provide the students with visual diagrams showing what is happening in terms of protons, neutrons, and electrons using + and - symbols. This would be the visual representation. Finally, the students could write a lab report explaining their understanding of these concepts. This would be the symbolic representation.

Attention Span

Middle grades teachers have firsthand experience with the short attention spans of young adolescents. The typical student has difficulty focusing on a single task for more than 15 minutes. However, there are educators who argue that if a variety of active learning approaches are employed, it is possible for middle grades students to attend for longer periods of time to something they believe is worthwhile and achievable (Brighton, 2007; Findley, 2005). Incorporating a variety of active learning strategies and moving between strategies during a lesson helps students to stay motivated and engaged.

Critical Thinking

Young adolescents are at the point in their development where they can begin thinking more abstractly and more logically, thus enabling them to think critically. To help students develop their critical thinking abilities, teachers must engage them in complex problems that require them to analyze, evaluate, and synthesize. They must ask students to answer questions and complete tasks at the higher levels of Bloom's Taxonomy. Middle grades students are also able to reason critically and move from "guessing to estimating, from preferring to evaluating, from grouping to classifying, from believing to assuming, from forming opinions without reasons to offering opinions with reasons, and from making judgments without criteria to making judgments with criteria" (Brighton, 2007, p. 13). Teachers can and should require middle grades students to think critically and to back up their conclusions with evidence.

Relevance

Making learning relevant to middle grades students is critical. Young adolescents are focused on the here-and-now and are frankly more concerned about who they will eat lunch with than about what they need to learn to prepare for high school or college. If they are told that the reason they need to learn a concept is that it will be on the end-of-year test or it will be something they need to know in the future, they are not particularly motivated to learn it. Active learning is a good approach to address this issue. If students are asked to engage in authentic, real-world projects, they will more readily see the relevance of what they are learning, which increases their motivation. "Providing students with opportunities to explore their own questions about themselves and the world in which they live is a sure way to ensure relevance in the curriculum" (Brighton, 2007, p. 9) and to engage young adolescents.

Creativity

Creativity is important, not only to us as individuals, but to us as a society. We need creative people to generate new and unique solutions to the problems that have plagued our world for some time as well as the new problems that are on the horizon. One need only look at the field of technology to see the power of creativity. Yet, the standardized testing culture in our schools seems to have stifled the fostering of creativity in our classrooms. Middle grades students are particularly vulnerable because they are increasingly concerned about being laughed at by their peers for "out of the box" thinking. Middle grades teachers need to be sensitive to this issue and provide students with regular opportunities to be creative through active learning projects, and they need to continually encourage creativity in their students. Hallman (1967) offers these techniques for teachers to encourage creative thinking:

- Encourage self-initiated learning.

- Encourage students to become deeply knowledgeable about subjects of interest.

- Defer judgments—don't give up on novel ideas too quickly.

- Be flexible in one's thinking.

- Ask lots of open-ended questions.

- Learn to cope with disappointment, frustration, and failure. (p. 330)

Questioning and Curiosity

Developmentally, middle grades students are at an interesting time in their lives when they have a greater awareness of the world outside of their classroom. They have an intense curiosity about that world and are beginning to ask questions to better understand how the world works. They have a greater ability to reflect and to consider their own views of events that happen around them. Middle grades students also tend to be idealistic and have a desire to change situations and to help those who are less fortunate than themselves. They become deeply concerned about any situation that they perceive lacks fairness. These typical characteristics of young adolescents lend themselves perfectly to active learning projects in which students search out information about societal problems, seek to understand those problems, begin to consider possible solutions, and act on some aspect of a given problem (Brighton, 2007; Nesin, 2012).

Middle grades students have an innate desire to understand their world. Young adolescents are becoming more and more aware of the world around them and are increasingly curious about how that world works (Brighton, 2007; Findley, 2005). Teachers should encourage students to ask questions and seek out answers about their physical world, the political world, various cultures, their own bodies, the technological world, and the business world. Using an active learning approach allows teachers to give students opportunities to ask questions themselves, rather than always answering the questions in the book or the questions the teacher asks them.

Constructivism

An important learning theory that underlies the idea of active learning is *constructivism*. While passive learning is generally associated with *behaviorism*, active learning is generally associated with constructivism. Therefore, it is important to explore some of the tenets of constructivism that undergird active learning. Underlying constructivist theory is the notion that the learner constructs his or her own understanding. Constructivism asserts that knowledge is actively constructed by the learner and not passively absorbed from another person. Knowledge cannot just be downloaded intact from the head of the teacher to the head of the student. Learners do not copy reality, but rather construct it. Learning is an active and constructive process that learners must be involved in. As learners we construct knowledge through activity with and reflection on the world around us (Byrnes, 2001; Narayan et al., 2013).

According to constructivist theory, each person has a cognitive web of knowledge. Ideas are not isolated from each other and stored within separate compartments in the brain, but instead are organized and associated with other understandings that one has encountered in the past. At any given time, understandings are organized as a network in an existing knowledge base. But this knowledge base does not remain static. Learning is an adaptive process in which learners construct new ideas or concepts based on their current knowledge. We learn by connecting new understandings together with what we already understand, and we modify our cognitive web or *schema*. New information is connected to prior knowledge and linked to prior experiences (Byrnes, 2001; Narayan et al., 2013; Petress, 2008).

Sensory experience and reason are the agents through which young adolescents construct new understandings. Constructivist theory suggests that young adolescents use intuition and reasoning to develop ideas before they are told rules to follow by adults. Piaget (1972) argues that this is done through three constructs that interact to influence learning. *Assimilation* is the notion of incorporating new information into one's existing knowledge base. Sometimes this new information is incompatible with the existing knowledge base and creates a state of *disequilibrium*. If this occurs, *accommodation* changes that existing knowledge base in order to assimilate the new information.

Cross (1991) explains it this way, "Learning is not so much an additive process, with new learning simply piling up on top of existing knowledge, as it is an active, dynamic process in which the connections are constantly changing and the structure reformatted" (p. 8).

Vygotsky (1962) claims that there is a zone of proximal development within which learning occurs. The *zone of proximal development* is that place between where a student can perform a skill independently and where the student can perform a skill with some assistance from a teacher or in collaboration with a peer. To assist a student who is constructing a new understanding that is within his or her zone of proximal development, the teacher or fellow student might use *scaffolding* as a means to offer support as the student advances to the next level of performance (Byrnes, 2001).

What does constructivist theory mean for teachers and students? Because student learning is built through one's own cognitive web and linked to prior experiences, it is, by nature, individual. Teachers cannot simply transfer their own webs of understanding to their students. Students must actively engage in learning and construct their own understanding. In constructivist theory, the emphasis is on learning and not teaching. Teachers who implement active learning strategies endeavor to provide students with learning opportunities that challenge their current understandings. Teachers serve as guides as their students develop concepts and experience the power of thinking for themselves. They provide students with situations that challenge the students' current knowledge base, putting them in a state of disequilibrium, and requiring them to accommodate and assimilate new understandings. It is important for teachers to give students time for reflection, so they can sort things out as they restructure old ways of thinking and move on to new understandings (Meyers & Jones, 1993). Teachers must be sure that these activities they provide for their students are within their zones of proximal development and be ready to provide the necessary scaffolding the students may need to construct their own understanding. This scaffolding may come from the teacher, but it may very well come from peers as students collaborate together.

In the end, it is important for the learner to take control of his or her own learning. Students need to be given the tools to use resources to discover the key ideas, to know when they understand, and to discern when they need more information and how to get that information (Bransford, Brown, & Cocking, 2003). This is intellectually active learning.

Socially Active Learning

At no point in their lives are people as concerned about their friends and their peers as they are during the time of early adolescence. While still valuing their parents, teachers, and other adults, those people take a back seat to the views of their peers. Young adolescents have a strong need to belong to a group and they search for social position within their peer group (Scales, 2010). Young adolescents often report that the most important reason for going to school is to be with their friends (Brighton, 2007). Since middle grades students are so peer-oriented, why not harness this desire for good? Teachers can turn this focus on peers to their advantage and use it to help students learn academically by allowing students to work together in their learning.

Constructivists often stress the importance of social construction in knowledge acquisition. According to Vygotsky (1962), higher cognitive functions occur first at an interpsychological level before the individual internalizes knowledge. Vygotsky believed that communication and negotiation of concepts with others are critical to student learning. Certainly, listening is an important part of the learning process, but so is talking. Students can process information as they talk it out with peers and negotiate meanings together (Meyers & Jones, 1993). Meaningful learning is facilitated by articulating explanations, whether to one's self, peers, or teachers (Michael, 2006).

Democratic education is another compelling reason for encouraging middle grades students to be socially active in the classroom. Classrooms that encourage students to be engaged in discourse while considering opposing viewpoints in a civil manner are assisting those students in becoming active members of our democratic society. It is important for middle grades students to really listen to the ideas of others, consider ideas intellectually, look for evidence to support or discredit different claims, introduce an opposing point of view in a productive way, analyze data together, and support their own opinions with evidence. Perhaps if students do this during the time of early adolescence, they will be better equipped to make informed decisions and convince others of their point of view as adults (Apple & Beane, 2007; Edwards, 2014).

Socially active learning can take a variety of forms. It could be two students working together as partners to complete a task, giving each other support and clarifying ideas as needed. It could be a small group of three or four students working together on a project, or discussing an open-ended question about a novel. It could be a teacher-led, whole class discussion in which students exchange ideas and use evidence to support their opinions.

David and Roger Johnson, who are known for their cooperative learning model, have identified five critical aspects of properly functioning cooperative groups:

1. *Positive interdependence*—group members need each other to succeed.

2. *Individual and group accountability*—each member is held accountable individually as well as for how their group performs.

3. *Face-to-face interaction*—by working with a smaller number of people, students are able to test ideas and receive feedback.

4. *Social skills*—teachers teach the social skills that are

necessary for middle grades students to successfully
work together.

5. *Group processing*—teachers allot time for team
members to process how well they are functioning as
a group and to troubleshoot problems (Fredrickson,
Dunlap, & McMahan, 2013).

Whether the cooperative learning model is used or students
work collaboratively in small groups, middle grades students
need to be socially active while learning. Of course, there
should be times of individual work in a middle grades
classroom, but some time should be set aside to allow
students to learn together, explore new ideas collaboratively,
develop respect for the ideas of others, hear the perspective
of diverse classmates, and develop socially while learning
academics (Nesin, 2012).

Physically Active Learning

Physically active learning is another category of active
learning to consider for middle grades students. Young
adolescents need opportunities to move, stretch, manipulate
objects related to their learning, release energy, and be
involved in hands-on activities (Nesin, 2012). This might be
done through manipulatives in a mathematics classroom,
experiments in a science classroom, drama in a language
arts classroom, or role-playing in a social studies classroom.
Options for getting students physically active while learning
are many and varied.

There are some physiological reasons that young
adolescents need to be physically active in the classroom.
First, the endocrine system, which regulates hormones, is

in development and still stabilizing. It is not uncommon for hormones to stimulate the adrenal glands of a young adolescent to produce a surge of adrenaline (Brighton, 2007). Adrenaline surges cause quick bursts of energy and strength. This causes an urge to move, which is not problematic if the student is already doing an activity that allows for movement rather than sitting still at a desk completing a worksheet. Adolescent boys can have as many as five to seven surges of testosterone every day. Testosterone encourages a quick tension release and leads to impulsivity, which, depending on the action of the boy, can be problematic in the middle of a class lesson (Walsh, 2004). While their metabolic system is stabilizing, young adolescents may move from periods of extreme restlessness to alternate periods of total fatigue where they sleep for inordinate periods of time (Caissy, 1994 Kellough & Kellough, 2008). Either of these extremes can be a problem in the middle of a class lesson; therefore, incorporating physical movement into instruction can be helpful.

A second physiological reason that causes restlessness in young adolescents is the fact that during this period of development the last three vertebrae fuse together to form the coccyx or the tailbone (Brighton, 2007). In some cases, this makes the area tender or sore making it difficult for the adolescent to sit for long periods of time, especially on hard surfaces such as the typical student desk seat (Caissy, 1994). This discomfort can be minimized if students are allowed to move while completing learning activities.

Parents and teachers often see a slowdown in learning capacity for young adolescents due to short attention spans and difficulty with concentration (Caissy, 1994). Young adolescents generally have a 10–15 minute attention span, and attention to one task drops off considerably after 10 minutes (Medina, 2014). One method teachers can use to account for this characteristic of young adolescents is to change activities during a lesson every 10–15 minutes, using a variety of instructional strategies or alternating between two instructional strategies in 10- to 15-minute intervals. Movement can help as well.

Physical activity can enhance student engagement because it increases their energy as they move. The higher the level of student engagement, the higher the likelihood of learning. Jensen (2005) explains the reason in terms of oxygen: "Oxygen is essential for brain function, and enhanced blood flow increases the amount of oxygen transported to the brain. Physical activity is a reliable way to increase blood flow, and hence oxygen, to the brain" (p. 62). Jensen (2005) also notes, "Amazingly, the part of the brain that processes movement is the same part of the brain that processes learning" (p. 61).

Of course middle school students do not need to move every minute of every class period, but incorporating some physical activity into lessons is important. As with every active learning strategy, it is important that the physical movement is purposeful and linked to the learning objectives. Movement for movement's sake is not the goal, but rather physical activity that supports learning.

Conclusion

This chapter has laid the groundwork of the theory that underlies active learning in middle grades classrooms. You may also want to look at the research appendix, which lists research studies that offer compelling evidence supporting the use of active learning with middle grades students. The active learning framework that incorporates three dimensions of active learning-intellectual, social, and physical-will be the framework that organizes this book. In later chapters you will learn practical strategies for implementing these different methods of active learning in the classroom. Ideally, you will discover strategies that incorporate more than one type of active learning simultaneously and you will feel equipped to engage your students in active learning in every lesson.

Chapter 2

Intellectually Active
Instructional Strategies

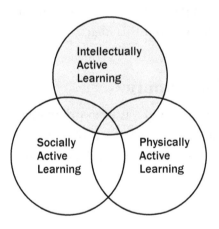

Nothing saddens me as much as witnessing brilliant young intellects addressing enormous efforts to trivial problems.
~Solomon Snyder

What do we mean by intellectually active? More than simply memorizing and regurgitating information, intellectually active students must be thinking at a higher level. Because the information available to us as a society is growing exponentially, it is increasingly important that students have a conceptual understanding of the content they are learning so they can sort, categorize, and prioritize that information. Learning endless facts is less important than understanding the ideas behind those facts. And it is not how much they know, but rather what they can do with that knowledge that matters. It is critical for students to be able to learn on their own and to apply that knowledge in new ways to solve new problems (Wagner, 2012). Brain research shows that when students are faced with unknown problems, their brains attempt to find connections to make sense of the problem. "The more complex the problem, the more complex the brain activity becomes" (Fogarty, 2009, p. 154), and this is when real learning occurs. Bloom's Taxonomy is a framework that helps us think about this idea.

Bloom's Taxonomy

Benjamin Bloom created a framework in 1956 to represent levels of thinking. These six levels of mental skills or abilities were revised in 2001 by Lorin Anderson and David Krathwohl (see Figure 4).

Figure 4: Revised Bloom's Taxonomy

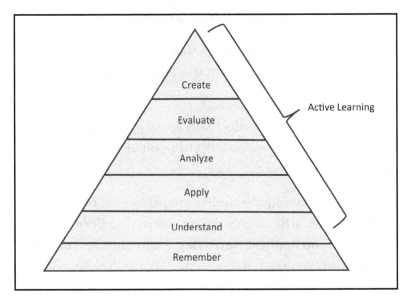

Remember—On this lowest level on Bloom's Taxonomy, students memorize and recall information previously provided to them. While this does require some cognitive effort, students working at this level are not considered intellectually active.

Understand—At this level, students understand concepts and are able to explain those concepts. Students simply understanding a new idea but not doing anything with it is passive rather than active learning. However, if students explain that concept in their own words and demonstrate their understanding, intellectual activity is beginning.

Apply—Students apply the concept, knowledge, or idea in a new way at this level, which definitely falls within the realm of intellectually active learning.

Analyze—In this level of intellectual activity, students distinguish between the different parts of an idea.

Evaluate—Based on knowledge they have learned, students justify a stance or a decision in this level of intellectually active learning.

Create—This level of intellectually active learning requires students to create a new product or point of view based on what they have learned.

So, activities that require students to perform at the top four levels of Bloom's Taxonomy are considered intellectually active. Students applying, analyzing, evaluating, and creating are definitely engaged in intellectual activity. The second (understanding) level of Bloom's, is considered intellectually active if students explain what they understand in a new or different way that demonstrates their understanding. To see what this looks like in the classroom, let us take a look into Mrs. Jones' and Mrs. Craver's classrooms. Both teachers are teaching eighth grade language arts and are working on gerunds, infinitives, and participles.

Intellectually Active Learning Approach Mrs. Jones' Classroom	Intellectually Passive Learning Approach Mrs. Craver's Classroom
Mrs. Jones has introduced the terms *gerund, infinitive,* and *participle.* She has asked the students to identify examples in sentences she has placed on the board. Now she sends the students off to work with a partner to write three sentences related to the novel they are reading. One sentence will contain a gerund, one will contain an infinitive, and one will contain a participle. Once students have written the sentences, each set of partners exchanges their sentences with another set of partners who must identify the correct verb in the three sentences. When considering Bloom's Taxonomy, Mrs. Jones is determining if her students *understand* the three concepts by asking them to apply them in a new sentence. She has engaged them in active learning.	Mrs. Craver has introduced the terms *gerund, infinitive,* and *participle.* She has asked the students to identify examples in sentences she has placed on the board. Now she passes out a worksheet with a list of 25 sentences. Each sentence has an underlined word. Beside each sentence the students are to write whether the underlined word is a gerund, infinitive, or participle. When considering Bloom's Taxonomy, Mrs. Craver is checking to see if her students *understand* the concepts by having them identify them in sentences. She has not yet engaged her students in active learning.

Getting students to be intellectually active in your classroom requires taking students to a higher level of thinking. Recall and comprehension do not count as being intellectually active.

Our goal is for our students to think critically—to engage in analysis, synthesis, and application. To be successful in our changing society, our students need to be prepared to do the hard work of thinking and to engage in problem solving and answering difficult questions. When we talk about intellectually active instructional strategies, the focus should be on the intellectually active part, not the strategy part. Having students complete activities is not the goal. The goal is critical thinking. As with every instructional decision you make in your classroom, the activity should enhance the learning of your content objectives.

This chapter describes various strategies to get students intellectually engaged in your content. Any of these strategies can be used to teach different content in various subject areas. Be flexible with the strategies and adapt them to suit your purposes and your style. Students could complete these activities individually, or if you want to intersect with the socially active dimension on the Active Learning Framework, you could have students work collaboratively on these activities.

Increasing Depth and Complexity

Kaplan's Depth and Complexity Model (Kaplan & Cannon, 2001) can be a useful tool for adding challenge to tasks by requiring students to be more intellectually active. Consider adding one of the aspects below to a question or prompt that you assign. After exploring resources you provide, students could answer the question in writing, or they could discuss the question in small groups or as a whole class.

- **Over Time**—Ask students to look at relationships between past, present, and future related to a specific concept.

- **Points of View**—Ask students to write from multiple perspectives or opposing viewpoints.

- **Interdisciplinary Connections**—Ask students to discuss relationships across disciplines.

- **Trends**—Ask students to determine factors that influence events or patterns.

- **Unanswered Questions**—Ask students to look at ambiguities or gaps of information in a topic.

- **Big Ideas**—Ask students to make generalizations and to distinguish principles.

- **Ethics**—Ask students to consider controversies related to a concept or to look for bias.

Venn Diagrams

John Venn proposed the Venn diagram in 1880 (Venn, 1880). The idea is that two circles (or more) overlap with one circle representing all of the possible members (or characteristics) of the set of a given concept and the other circle representing all of the possible members (or characteristics) of the set of another concept. Where the two circles overlap are the members (or characteristics) of both sets. Teachers can incorporate this good tool into any content area by asking students to compare and contrast different concepts related to a given topic.

Students can use pencils and do this activity in their notebooks, use chart paper and markers to display their diagrams for the class, or use computers or tablets. Select two or three concepts that can be compared and contrasted. The number of concepts corresponds to the number of circles in the diagram. Explain that the students should think of as many characteristics or ideas related to each of the listed concepts as they can.

Have students locate the area where the circles overlap, indicating characteristics that the two concepts have in common. The outer parts of each circle represent the contrasting characteristics unique to each concept. Challenge students to think of characteristics that are more subtle, characteristics that require inferences, or characteristics that are implicit rather than explicit.

Practical Suggestions

- Two websites with free interactive Venn diagrams are classtools.net and readwritethink.org.

- Have small groups make Venn diagrams using two hula hoops and characteristics that are written on cards.

- Use an interactive board with characteristics already listed outside of the circles. Students take turns coming to the board and dragging the characteristics to the proper location in the Venn diagram. Allow them to move words already placed by previous students and have discussions about the discrepancies.

- For students' first Venn diagram: First think of one characteristic for each region of the diagram as a class and then have the students continue on their own.

Here is an example of a Venn diagram using some of the ideas we learned in Chapter One about active and passive learning:

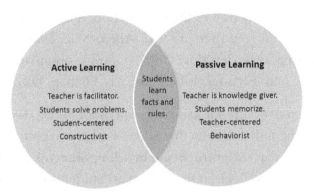

Concept Maps and Graphic Organizers

Concept maps and graphic organizers (Novak & Gowin, 1996; Vanides, Yin, Tomita, & Ruiz-Primo, 2005) are visual representations of a topic with bubbles representing different concepts or ideas and lines between the bubbles representing connections among related ideas. Concept maps are graphical tools that organize and structure knowledge and display relationships between terms. They allow students to visualize how individual ideas are part of a larger whole and illuminate big ideas. They provide spatial arrangements that represent the conceptual organization of a text (Merchie & Van Keer, 2013). Concept maps give students opportunities to think about connections, organize their thoughts, and reflect on what they understand about a topic. This instructional strategy aligns with a constructivist approach because concept mapping assists students in connecting new ideas into the schema in their mind of previously learned ideas related to the topic.

There are several benefits to using concept maps and graphic organizers with middle grades students. They increase thinking skills because they allow students to break information into manageable chunks. Since they are creating a picture of the information, images are more easily remembered than just text (Allen, 2008; Feinstein, 2009; Gregory & Herndon, 2010). "Graphic organizers make thinking and learning visible" (Fogarty, 2009, p. 112).

The ideal structure for using concept maps in the classroom is an open-ended activity that allows students to construct their own map structure. Begin by asking students to select the key terms of a given topic, then ask students to categorize those terms and consider the relationships among them. Each student or group of students will likely end up constructing a different map, but the individual maps give the teacher an opportunity to see the connections students have made about the ideas that they are learning.

Practical Suggestions

- Technology tools such as inspiration.com and bubbl.us help students create concept maps using computers or tablets.

- Use chart paper, sticky notes, and markers to create concept maps. Students can use sticky notes to move terms around as they consider relationships among ideas.

- Students can use dry-erase boards to easily make changes without making too much of a mess.

Here is an example of a concept map using the information in Chapter One about active learning:

Problem-Based Learning

The idea of problem-based learning actually began in medical education (Neufeld & Barrows, 1974) and has become a successful active learning model in middle grades education (Kilbane & Milman, 2014). Problem-based learning is a student-centered approach that allows students to learn content knowledge while using academic skills and problem-solving strategies to solve authentic real-world problems that are loosely structured. The focus in the classroom moves from teaching to learning. The teacher moves from knowledge-deliverer to facilitator of knowledge (Fredrickson, McMahan, Dunlap, 2013).

The first task of the teacher is to give students an authentic, real-world problem to solve that has one or more solutions. Teachers create the problem in such a way that students will develop content knowledge and skills while reaching a solution. Middle grades students are motivated to learn when they are asked to solve problems that are relevant and important to them. But those problems need to be appropriate in size and scope to foster curiosity. A benefit of the problem-based learning model is that it fosters development of students' critical thinking and problem-solving skills, which are important lifelong skills.

The teacher's role does not end after selecting the problem to assign. Once the students receive the problem, ensure that everyone understands the problem, scaffold the work, and guide them through important steps. Students must identify what they already know, what they need to know, and where they might find information they need. One of the teacher responsibilities is making appropriate resources available by creating a list of acceptable websites to explore or directing students toward resources such as books, periodicals, and content experts. Students identify possible solutions, try out solutions, collect data, and evaluate their ideas. Once students believe they have a viable solution and have evidence to support that their solution is now or will be successful, they present that solution, usually as some sort of product (Fredrickson, McMahan, Dunlap, 2013).

Practical Suggestions

- One structure for problem-based learning is a webquest. This is a teacher-created website that has the problem, the guidelines, and the task all in one place and directs students to pre-selected, approved websites for the information they will need to solve the problem. Find more information about webquests at webquest.org or zunal.com.

- Middle grades students need structure to organize their work on an open-ended problem. Give deadlines for different parts of the process. For example, "You need to explore three resources by 11:15 a.m.".

- Think ahead of time about how you will scaffold your students when they get stuck. One good strategy is to have pre-planned questions that foster student thinking or direct their focus to a particular aspect of the problem. Often a counterexample can be helpful in getting students off a non-productive path.

- If this is a strategy that is of interest to you, do not try to reinvent the wheel. There are many good resources available to you and a quick Internet search can lead you to well-developed problems aligned with your content as well as support for you as the teacher.

Puzzles

Puzzles can be a fun way to add challenge to a concept and require students to become more intellectually active. The key to this strategy is careful selection of a puzzle. Puzzles such as word searches, which ask students to find words in a square of random letters, do not require higher-level thinking. The Internet is a good source for endless puzzles that require critical thinking related to your content area.

Practical Suggestion

- Place puzzles in folders in a box in a corner of the room. As students finish classwork or tests early, they can select a folder puzzle and work on it until they solve it.

High Level Questioning

It is more interesting for middle grades students if they are asked to answer high quality questions that are worthy of exploration rather than only answering low-level questions with an obvious correct answer. High level questions such as those that correlate with the "apply, analyze, and create" levels of Bloom's Taxonomy challenge students to be intellectually active. As a teacher you want to select questions that require students to think critically, to wrestle with the issues in your content, and to think deeply about what they are learning.

Edwards (2014) suggests three categories for high-level questions:

Category 1: How Do We Make Sense of This?

Questions that fall into this category require students to examine resources on a particular topic and make sense of it. Students synthesize by putting ideas together in a new way; analyze essential concepts and themes; understand causes, reasons, or methods of what has occurred; compare and contrast ideas; and classify ideas into categories. The following question stems are some examples that could be applied to any content area.

Synthesis

What are the major themes of the passage?

I only know about _____. How would you explain _____ to me?

Under what conditions is _____ true or not true?

What conjectures can you make?

Is there a general rule?

Analysis

What is the main point of the author's argument?
How does he support it?

What evidence is given to show that ____?

How would you explain it in a simpler way?

How can we categorize these ideas?

Compare and Contrast

What do ____ and ____ have in common?

What is the difference between ____ and ____?

Causes/Results/Process

What are the procedures or processes?

What are the major causes of this situation?

Suppose ____ happened; what would be the
consequences?

What are ways that ____ have impacted ____?

Category 2: What do we think about this?

Questions in this category ask students to react to
information they have. They require students to do things
like make interpretations, make inferences, or evaluate
something based on established criteria. The following

question stems for this category are general examples that could be applied to any content area.

Interpretation and Inference

> What does the author mean when he says _____?
>
> How would this look to a _____?
>
> What would _____ mean from the viewpoint of _____?
>
> Why do you think the author wrote this?

Evaluation

> Is there a better solution to _____?
>
> What is the value of _____?
>
> Do you agree with the actions of _____?
>
> Would it be better if _____?

Category 3: How can we use this?

Questions in this category require students to consider how particular information can be used. They require students to apply knowledge to a different context, make recommendations, transfer what they are learning to new problems or situations, and use the knowledge to solve a problem. The following question stems for this category are general examples that could be applied to any content area.

Application

> What would happen if there were no _____?
>
> What would happen if _____ were true?

What if we changed _____?

How does this relate to _____?

Problem Solving

Suppose you were in _____ situation. How will this concept impact your actions?

How many ways can you come up with to _____?

Suppose _____ were to happen. How would you solve it?

Based on what you know, how would you _____? (Edwards, 2014, p. 19-23).

Practical Suggestions

- When discussing high-level questions with a class, keep the question posted at the front of the room.

- Have someone, either the teacher or a student, write a running list of ideas on the board. This helps to keep students focused on the question at hand and helps to eliminate repetition and needless rabbit trails. It also requires students to go deeper into the content if they are required to add more ideas to the list.

Chain Note

The Chain Note strategy (Angelo & Cross, 1993) requires students to respond in multiple ways to a question, in other words, you cannot repeat the answer someone else in your group gave. You must either go deeper or broader. The strategy encourages students to dig deeper and not just scratch the surface with an easy response.

The teacher arranges the students into rows or groups of equal numbers (e.g., six groups of five students). The teacher passes out sheets with questions written on them so that each student in each group gets one of five different questions. The students individually answer the question they have been given in writing. After a sufficient amount of time has passed, the teacher asks the students to pass their papers to the next person in the group. The students then add something new to what the person before them wrote. The process repeats until everyone has answered all five questions. Once this has been done, the teacher leads a whole class discussion about each of the questions.

Practical Suggestions

- Consider printing the questions on different colored sheets of paper. That will help you track the progress of the chain notes and also eliminate confusion about which question is being discussed by the whole group. "Let's talk about the blue question now..."

- Asking students to share something from their papers takes pressure off the student since he or she is sharing something a group member said and not necessarily his or her own idea. This works great for getting students to participate who are normally reluctant to share their own thoughts.

- If you want to use the chain notes as formative assessment data, have students write their names beside the comments.

Newsletters or Blogs

Asking students to create a newsletter that incorporates the important ideas in the content you are studying can be both motivating and a method of getting students intellectually active. There are many ways to construct a newsletter. First, select an audience for the students. Parents could be the audience for a monthly or quarterly publication in which students explain the nuances of what they have learned in the previous month. Or a specific newsletter could be written with an imaginary audience in mind. For example, it could be a newsletter that a historical figure might have written to his or her country after a specific event. Give students specific requirements for the number of articles to include and the number of perspectives to represent. Including articles written from different points of view will challenge students intellectually. Give students enough parameters to ensure that they include all of the important content information, and at the same time challenge students to higher level thinking, not just a regurgitation of the facts.

Middle grades students are also accustomed to the idea of blogs and they can reach the same content goals by creating a blog that incorporates the key content information.

Practical Suggestions

- For newsletters, use Microsoft Publisher or similar software or an online tool such as weebly.com.

- An easy blogging tool for classrooms is edublogs.org.

Write a Song or Poem

Because it is of great interest to many middle grades students, music is a good tool you can use to motivate them to be intellectually active. Ask students to write and perform a song or poem about the content you are studying. The key is setting requirements that challenge students to higher level thinking rather than just regurgitating the facts. Create an assignment sheet with specific requirements and detailed information about how the song or poem will be evaluated. For example, if studying a historical figure, the song or poem might have to include three relationships, two major life events, and how the person might hope a situation is resolved. Perhaps your directions might require two characters singing from different perspectives regarding an issue. This is an excellent strategy to encourage creativity in your students.

Practical Suggestions

- To save class time and the awkwardness of performing in front of peers on cue, students can make video recordings of themselves at home that can be played in class the next day.

- If you regularly incorporate into your classes some of the many content-related songs found on youtube.com, this strategy will not be a foreign concept to your students.

Metaphors and Analogies

Another method to get your students intellectually active is to ask them to create metaphors, analogies, and similes relating the concept they are learning about to another concept. All three of these literary devices require students to make comparisons, but there are differences.

- Metaphors compare two ideas that are seemingly unrelated without using *like* or *as*; for example, comparing cultures in the United States to a salad. We all live together, but different cultures provide a different flavor to the overall experience.

- A simile makes a comparison between two ideas using *like* or *as*. For example, my life is like a ping pong game.

- Analogies use the pattern "*a* is to *b* as *c* is to *d*." For example, pencil is to paper as paintbrush is to canvas.

Metaphors, similes, and analogies cause students to think deeply about a concept and its characteristics. They can also reveal understandings as well as misconceptions in student thinking (Caine, Caine, McClintic, & Klimek, 2009; Gregory & Herndon, 2010).

Practical Suggestion

- Provide scaffolding for your students to increase their likelihood of success. The first time you assign a metaphor, give them an example. Next, come up with one together as a whole class. Then have students come up with a metaphor in small groups. With the next concept, ask students to come up with individual metaphors.

Journal Writing

Journal writing is a good strategy to get students to explain their reasoning, which requires them to be intellectually active. Explaining their reasoning should be a normal expectation of students in your classroom. Regularly ask them to explain their reasoning for the conclusions they have drawn and have them provide evidence to support that reasoning. Expect this of students verbally during class discussions, and, more formally, give them journal prompts related to the content you are studying.

Practical Suggestions

- Assigning a journal prompt to a different class period each day of a given week gives you only one set of journals to grade in any given evening.

- Give students a simple rubric, show them examples of journal entries, and ask them to give each entry a rubric score. This helps students have a clearer understanding of your expectations. Here is a sample rubric I used for journals in my mathematics classroom:

4—Correct answer. Clear and complete explanation. Someone who doesn't know anything about the topic could figure it out. Includes a diagram if appropriate. Includes an example.

3—Correct answer. Clear explanation. Someone who knows about the topic could understand it. Might include a diagram or example.

2—Answer is incorrect or there is an insufficient explanation.

1—Incorrect answer and insufficient explanation.

Inquiry Learning

Inquiry learning has roots in constructivism and is a method of encouraging students to explore ideas and to construct an understanding of a particular concept for themselves. It is an approach that reverses the traditional structure of a lesson. Instead of the teacher providing students with the critical information related to a topic at the beginning of class and then giving students opportunities to practice that knowledge, the teacher's responsibility is to set up a structured task that leads students down the path of understanding. Much like scientific inquiry, students form and test hypotheses, collect data, and analyze their findings to draw conclusions. Students become actively involved in the creation of new knowledge and in their own learning. However, the idea of inquiry learning can be applied to other subjects, not just science. It is important to structure the task, question, problem, or scenario so that it is open-ended, yet not too vague. There need to be enough parameters to ensure that your students will uncover the important content information naturally as a part of their investigation.

Practical Suggestions

- The critical role of the teacher changes from the beginning of class to the end of class. At the end of the activity, it is important for the teacher to bring the ideas of the students together and ensure that all students have reached the same conclusions about the important concept under study. The teacher leads a discussion that includes that critical information, ideally coming from students rather than the teacher.

- Middle grades students need structure. Give them specific time limits and deadlines for different aspects of the activity.

- Prepare questions designed to scaffold students ahead of time. Predict points where they might get stuck and think of questions you can ask to prompt them in a productive direction.

Research Projects/Papers/Presentations

Frankly, we have saved the best for last. Projects are the most effective intellectually active strategy that can be used with middle grades students. Students are more motivated to dig in intellectually if they are completing a project or preparing for a presentation on a topic. Project-based learning engages students in real-world challenges and usually involves peer collaboration, critical thinking, communication skills, and interdisciplinary learning. In order for project-based learning to be done well it should have six key elements built into the design: academic rigor, authenticity, applied learning, active exploration, adult connections, and assessment (Lattimer & Riordan, 2011).

Ideally, you will be able to allow your students some choice in the topic. Not only is choice motivating but it also helps students make relevant connections. Seeing the relevance in their learning is especially critical to young adolescents and is supported by the curriculum principle in *This We Believe*: "Curriculum is challenging, exploratory, integrative, and relevant" (NMSA, 2010, p. 14). However, there are times that you may assign a topic and that is fine as well.

The key to success in engaging middle level students in projects is to provide an appropriate amount of structure. Breaking a large project into small chunks with deadlines is critical. For example, you might have deadlines for selecting a topic, writing questions that they want to know about the topic, researching the topic, outlining the presentation, or storyboarding the project.

A formal presentation is important as a culminating event for many reasons. The presentation requires students to summarize and synthesize the important information they have learned. Also, the other students need to learn from their peers. Finally, the final presentation provides both accountability and motivation to work hard on the project.

There are many benefits of projects, not the least of which is creativity. Our classrooms have become too regulated in the current climate of testing and accountability, and projects allow middle grades students the opportunity to once again display their creativity. They also create memories. If you think about what you learned during your school years, the things that would stand out the most are projects that you did in different classes. "Projects are what students remember long after the bell rings. Great teachers know that their highest calling is to make memories" (Martinez & Stager, 2013, p. 67).

Practical Suggestions

- Do not try to reinvent the wheel...it is not necessary to come up with the projects you want your students to complete. There are many good resources on the Internet. For example, the New York City Department of Education has published a helpful document about project-based learning in middle school: http://schools.nyc.gov/documents/teachandlearn/ project_basedfinal.pdf

- Some good technologies that students can use to create visual aids are:

  - prezi.com

  - edu.glogster.com

  - voicethread.com

  - haikudeck.com

  - educreations.com

Conclusion

Information is the fastest growing commodity in our society, and the amount of knowledge we possess in our world is doubling every year. It is obvious that our middle grades students cannot possibly memorize every piece of information they will need to use in their lives. It is just not possible. What would be more helpful to prepare our students for their unpredictable life paths is to help them become critical thinkers and problem solvers. We need to teach students to be intellectual risk-takers and to not fear open-ended, unknown problems.

By requiring your students to be intellectually active while learning your content, you are helping them learn important skills in the process. Intellectually active strategies empower students to research ideas, determine the relevant information, and verify the credibility of that information. Active learning that engages the intellect helps students make sense of the changing world around them. Finally, intellectually active learning helps develop the skills of synthesizing and presenting what they have learned to convince others of the value of that information. Simply, getting your students intellectually active in your classroom prepares them for life.

Chapter 3
Socially Active Instructional Strategies

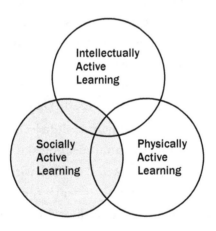

*We should not only use the brains we have, but all
that we can borrow. ~Woodrow Wilson*

Anyone who has spent time with middle grades students
will quickly agree that young adolescents are, by nature,
social. They love to talk and they value their peers highly
(Caissy, 1994). Why not capture this enthusiasm and use it
to your advantage in getting them to learn your content?

When students work in small groups and engage in conversation about the content, they are participating in socially active learning. Socially active learning allows thinking to become audible and public (Fogarty, 2009). It requires students to solidify their thoughts and organize them to the point that they can explain their thinking to someone else. Allowing students to become socially active in the classroom gives students the opportunity to exchange ideas and to defend the way they think (Gregory & Herndon, 2010). Whole class and small group discussions foster understanding for both the speaker and the listener (Fogarty, 2009).

Improvements and new types of technological devices continue to change patterns and ways of communication for young adolescents outside of the classroom. Middle grades students are comfortable communicating via social media and many, if not most, young adolescents prefer texting to talking (Igel & Urquhart, 2012). While acknowledging this preference, teachers can still help middle level students develop their face-to-face communication skills by teaching them appropriate ways to talk and to work with others. Not only will this benefit their ability to learn the content at hand, but it will assist them in future work environments (Hansen & Hansen, 2010).

The following strategies are designed to encourage socially active learning and to leverage the desire of middle grades students to work together. Any of these strategies can be used to teach different content in various subject areas. Be flexible with the strategies and adapt them to suit your purposes and your style. Please leave classroom management concerns on the back burner until you have a chance to read Chapter 12 when we will discuss strategies for managing student behavior and keeping them on task while working together.

Fishbowl

All the variations of the fishbowl strategy (Harris, 2011) have one thing in common—they engage students in actively learning together. First, picture a fish bowl or perhaps an aquarium. The people standing around the fishbowl are looking in and watching the fish interact but are not interacting with the fish themselves. The fish are interacting with each other but are oblivious to the people watching them.

To bring the fishbowl analogy into the classroom, the teacher divides the students into two concentric circles, an inner circle (the fish) and an outer circle (the spectators). The teacher poses a high-level, open-ended question and allows the inner circle of students to discuss the question while students in the outer circle listen quietly to their discussion. After an appropriate amount of time, the students switch roles. Students who began in the inner circle now move to the outer circle, and the students who began in the outer circle now move to the inner circle. The students who are now in the inner circle continue to discuss the same question adding more ideas and depth to what the first group discussed. Students who are now in the outer circle listen quietly as the students in the inner circle continue their discussion.

Practical Suggestions

- You have the option of being in the inner circle or the outer circle depending on the ability of the students to lead their own discussion while in the inner circle. The goal is to get them to the point that the teacher can stand quietly in the outer circle while the inner circle students facilitate their own conversation. Taking ownership of their learning helps middle grades students develop independence.

- Either use a timer for this activity or just let the discussion run its course before switching the inner and outer circles.

- Post the discussion question on the board for all to see, so the students can stay focused on the topic. Refer students to the question on the board if necessary to get them back on topic.

- For differentiation purposes, you might consider putting low-level and medium-level students in the inner circle first, and let your high-level students enter the inner circle last. It is more difficult to add on to what has been said and go deeper than it is to enter a discussion at the beginning.

Numbered Heads Together

In the Numbered Heads Together strategy (Edwards, 2014) the teacher arranges students in small groups and gives each member of the group a number. For example, if students are working in groups of three, one of the students is Number 1, one of the students is Number 2, and one of the students is Number 3. The teacher poses a question for the groups to discuss. The goal for the groups is for every member of the group to understand and be able to explain the answer that the group agrees upon. When the teacher brings the class back together for the whole class discussion, he or she selects a number at random. The students with that number are the representatives for their groups and report what their group discussed. This requires an element of accountability for all of the students in every group to be engaged because they do not know who will be called upon to report for the group.

Practical Suggestions

- Use colored squares with numbers to put students in groups efficiently. So, for example, there is a red #1, red #2, red #3, and red #4. The four students who have received red cards find each other and work in the same group. Four other students receive numbered blue cards, four students receive numbered green cards, and so forth.

- Post the question being discussed on the board for all to see, so the students can stay focused on the topic. You can refer students to the question on the board if necessary to get them back on track.

6-3-1

This strategy (Edwards, 2014) has three simple steps and takes place after students have read a common text. First, ask students to write six important points or key ideas from the selected reading. The teacher gives students an appropriate amount of time to do this individually. Second, arrange students into groups of three and ask them to select from the ideas on all of the group members' lists the three most important ideas. Third, ask the groups to select one key idea from their list of three to share with the class.

- List on the board the key idea shared from each group. This serves two purposes. First, it keeps groups from repeating what other groups before them have shared. Second, students can take notes on these key ideas.

- Consider displaying a timer to help students pace themselves during each of the three phases of this strategy.

Bone to Pick with You

This strategy (Edwards, 2014) encourages students to ask their own questions about what they want to learn. The teacher prints out sheets of paper with a picture of a dog bone on each. Each student is given a sheet and asked to individually write a question about the content they are learning on the dog bone. Students do not write their names on the sheets. After collecting all the questions, the teacher places them face down in a pile at a designated place in the classroom. Next, the teacher arranges students into small groups, and one representative from each group randomly selects two bones from the pile and takes the sheets back to the group. The group then selects one of the two questions that they wish to discuss or explore. Once the group believes that they have "gnawed" the bone clean by thoroughly discussing the question, they can share their thoughts with the entire class during the whole class discussion.

Practical Suggestions

- If you are concerned about the quality of questions the students might ask, have them write their questions at the end of class one day. As you review the questions before class begins the next day, remove questions that are inappropriate for discussion and ones that are duplicates. Or, if you see a question that puzzles or interests several students, you can select that one for the entire class to gnaw on. Another option is to assign certain questions to certain groups for differentiation purposes.

- You can also write a question or two on the bones if you have something in particular you want the groups to discuss.

- When a group is sharing what they discussed, display the question on the document camera for all the groups to see.

Small Group Projects

An important method for getting middle grades students socially active as they learn is small group projects, which is how work gets done in many places of business and industry. Small group projects can range in terms of scope and time allotted, but they are engaging to middle level students and valuable as a learning strategy. The groups can be as small as partners, but I do not recommend having more than four in a group. Five could work if they are students who are used to working in small groups. For middle grades students to be successful in completing small group projects, the teacher must provide structure by setting guidelines and parameters including giving them timelines with built-in deadlines for different aspects of the project. At the same time, give your students as much autonomy and independence as they can handle. Give them choice where you can. Perhaps they can select the topic of focus, or perhaps they can select the method in which they present their findings. Students will amaze you as they benefit from the synergy of collaborating on something of interest.

Practical Suggestions

- Middle grades students need structure. Break the project into small chunks and have deadlines for each of those chunks.

- Assign or let students choose some sort of an end product that demonstrates what they have learned.

- Consider having students complete a self-assessment and a peer-assessment at the end of the project. Ask questions about the specifics and quality of each group member's contribution. Have them reflect on how they could work better together in the future.

Jigsaw

The longevity of the Jigsaw strategy (Aronson, Blaney, Stephin, Sikes, & Snapp, 1978) is due to how well it works. In Jigsaw teachers assign students to expert groups and to home groups. Each expert group becomes an expert on some portion of the content the class is studying. Once the teacher decides the expert groups have had sufficient time to acquire their expertise, students go back into their home groups. Each home group has a representative from each expert group. Therefore, each member of a home group has a different area of expertise to share with their home group members. The students go around the circle and explain to their group what they learned while in their expert group.

Practical Suggestions

- Using a timer helps students gauge their progress.

- A structured handout guides students to identify key ideas. If they write notes on their guides while in the expert groups, they will more likely pass on the important information to their home groups.

- Assigning letters to the expert groups and numbers to the home groups makes it less confusing. For example, if a student gets assigned B-2, she is in expert group B and home group 2.

- Check in with the expert groups to ensure that they have a good handle on the key ideas before sending them back to their home groups.

Elevator Talk

This is a fun strategy (Edwards, 2014) that requires students to synthesize the most important ideas into a concise, yet informal presentation. Students are asked to problem solve an issue in small groups. They need to come up with arguments in favor of their solution or their position on an issue and practice a concise, 90-second argument for whatever their position is. After the groups have been given sufficient time to do this, the teacher takes on the role of an important official. Depending on the issue, this might be a school board member, the governor, the President, or a foreign leader. The group pretends to ride in an elevator with the important official who asks their opinion on the topic at hand. They have the 90 seconds that it takes to ride the elevator to the meeting where the decision will be made to convince the important official of their position.

Practical Suggestions

- Use a timer to keep track of the 90 seconds.

- You might need to make specific requirements, such as every member of the group has to make at least one statement on the elevator ride.

Think Pair Share

This is another strategy that numerous teachers have used over the years because it works so well. There are three steps to the process. The first step is the Think part of the process. The teacher poses a question and asks students to think individually about the answer using whatever resources the teacher designates. During the second step, Pair, students discuss their thoughts with a partner. During the third step, Share, the teacher leads a whole class discussion in which pairs of students share their ideas with the class.

Practical Suggestion

- It is a good idea to have regular assigned partners who are seated near each other so that a lot of class time is not wasted assigning partners or transitioning into the Pair step.

Word Sort

This is a great strategy (Spencer, 2008) to use when the students have read an assigned selection and you want to focus on vocabulary. The reading could come from a textbook, an article, a story—anything. During the first step in the process, the teacher provides each student with a stack of ten blank cards. Individually, the students select ten words or short phrases from the reading that they think are important. The teacher arranges students into small groups for the second step in which the small groups combine all the word cards the students in the group wrote. The group works together to arrange the cards into three or four categories and create a label for each of their categories. Once all of the groups have their categories, the teacher asks the groups to share their categories with the class and to share some representative words for each category. This is an opportunity to focus on some of the big ideas in the reading. Next, the teacher initiates the third step of the process by asking the groups to identify the five most important words from all of their cards. Once the groups have selected their five words, they move all of the other cards off to the side. In the fourth step of the process, students write one sentence using those five words. They record their sentence on a piece of paper so that it can be shared with the class during the whole class discussion, which is the final step. The class determines if the sentences they created are true statements based on the reading, they write the accurate statements on the board, and students write the statements in their notes.

Practical Suggestions

- The number of cards can vary: ten is not a firm number.

- Make a rule that "miscellaneous" cannot be a category. This will require them to grapple with the ideas of the reading in more depth.

- Display the directions for the steps one-at-a-time to prevent students from working ahead and missing the point of each step or skipping steps.

- Using markers to write the words on the cards makes sorting easier because the words are clearly visible to all group members.

Student-Led Questioning

This strategy (Edwards, 2014) is a good one for requiring all students to participate in small group discussions. The teacher creates questions on colored slips of paper. The number of questions should be the same as the number of students in each group. For example, if students are in groups of four, the teacher creates four questions, one on each of four colored sheets of paper. In their groups, each student has a different color paper with a question. Each student leads the group in discussing the question on his or her paper and writes the answers/conclusions/ideas of the group on that same paper. During the whole class discussion, the teacher calls on students with each color of paper to report what their group decided.

Practical Suggestion

- Use a timer to help the groups pace themselves. For example, tell them they have two minutes to discuss the purple question and set the timer. Then when the timer sounds, they move on to the green question, and discuss it for two minutes, etc.

Debates

What middle school students do not like to argue their point and stand their ground until they convince everyone that they are right? Debates can be structured formally or informally.

Although they can be done in small groups or with a whole class, typically teachers prefer small groups because they increase the opportunities for students to participate.

Middle grades students need guidance and structure to experience success with debating. First, students meet in small groups and list clear arguments with detailed evidence for each argument. Second, the teacher structures and facilitates the debate with time limits for each side to make their points. A facilitator monitors the debate.

Practical Suggestions

- Create a sheet with a t-chart with each position written at the top. Students write a list of points made on each side of the chart. They can add notes to their chart before, during, and after the debate. This adds an element of accountability and requires students to consider both points of view, something that young adolescents are developmentally just beginning to really be able to do. After the debate, students turn in their charts.

- It is critical to teach students how to disagree agreeably. Teach them phrases to say such as, "I understand your point, but I have a different view..." or "Another way to think about it might be..."

Round-Robin Brainstorming

This strategy (Putnum & Paulus, 2009) is designed to engage students in brainstorming in a fair and equitable manner. Structured to allow all students to participate and voice their ideas, one student does not dominate.

Teachers assign students to small groups of four to six members. The teacher poses an open-ended, divergent question with more than one possible answer. Each group chooses one member as the recorder who writes the group's ideas. The remaining group members offer ideas one-at-a-time as they go around in a clockwise direction. Each person offers an idea, which the recorder writes *without evaluation by the rest of the group*. The group members proceed to take turns offering their ideas. This process repeats several times around the circle until every member of the group has had multiple opportunities to share ideas or the group runs out of ideas or information to share.

Practical Suggestions

- If a group is having difficulty taking turns, have some object such as a squishy ball that the students must pass around in a clockwise direction. Only the student with the squishy ball is allowed to speak and others in the group cannot interrupt.

- Because this is a brainstorming activity, it is important for the teacher to emphasize that all ideas should be recorded without evaluation. Explain that to achieve a free-flowing exchange of ideas, the goal is to not inhibit students in sharing their thoughts for fear of judgment by their peers. Connect brainstorming to the creative process that real-life work teams use to generate the ideas that eventually solve critical problems.

- For an extension have students discuss, categorize, evaluate, and prioritize the ideas.

Three-Step Interview

There are many benefits to this strategy, which gets students actively engaged and talking to each other (Kagan, 2001). This strategy develops listening skills in students as well as the ability to consider another person's perspective. The process also helps students realize that some questions elicit better information than others and helps to develop questioning skills.

After the teacher arranges the students into groups of two, one partner interviews the other. The interviewing partner asks questions and then actively listens and paraphrases to the interviewee what he or she heard. During the second step of the process, the interviewer and interviewee exchange roles giving both students the opportunity to share their views, practice active listening, and really hear the viewpoints of another person. After both students have had the opportunity to be the interviewer, the teacher combines pairs of students into groups of four. While in their groups of four, the students share what they learned from their interviewee.

Practical Suggestions

- Most students will need additional structure. Display a class timer, designate an amount of time for each of the three steps in the process, and restart the timer between each step.

- Students could take notes of the interviewee's responses on a teacher-created note taking sheet.

Four-Corner Sticky Notes

This is a helpful strategy to get students considering possible alternatives to their own thinking. It requires students to compare their own solutions to solutions of their peers and to decide whether to take one student's solution path or to combine answers to produce the best possible answer. The teacher gives each student a sticky note. There are five different colors of sticky notes among the students so that they will be placed into groups of four with students who have the same colored sticky note (i.e., if there are 20 students, there will be five groups of four). First, the students work individually on a question or problem and write what they believe is the best answer on their own sticky note. Next, students get with other students who have the same color sticky note. Each group is given a sheet where they place the sticky notes of the four group members into the four corners. They must work together to examine and discuss their various answers to come up with what they believe is the best possible answer, which is written in the middle of the group sheet (Runde, 2013).

Conclusion

Any of the strategies in this chapter could be used in any content area. Any given strategy may be better for a particular topic or a lesson. Be flexible and adapt these strategies to fit your students' needs. They are not hard and firm procedures that cannot be changed. Use them the way they are written or use them as a springboard to develop your own method.Feel free to make them work for you and your students. The point is, get your students talking to each other about what they are learning. Take advantage of the social nature of young adolescents. We learn when we process information with others.

Chapter 4

Physically Active
Instructional Strategies

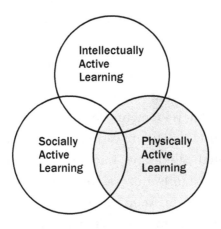

The mind can only absorb what the seat can endure.
~Anonymous

If you have been teaching middle school for more than
two days, you probably have experienced the frustration of
standing in front of 28 bored adolescents who are not paying
attention to you. At these moments, teachers use "tricks of
the trade" to get their students' attention. They might ask an

inattentive student a question for the purpose of shaming them into compliance while implying to the rest of the class that the same will happen to them if they do not begin paying attention. They might reward the attentive students and punish the inattentive ones. They might deliver the sermon about the importance of knowing this content because it will be on the test.

But there is a better method: use physical activity. According to the old adage you can lead a horse to water, but you can't make him drink. True, but you can give him a salt tablet so that he is thirsty enough to want to drink the water. Physical activity in the classroom is like that salt tablet. It gets unsuspecting students engaged, and dare I say, having fun while learning the content you have been so desperately trying to drill into their heads. And here is a well-kept secret…not only will the kids have more fun, you will too.

Chapter 1 discussed that young adolescents' bodies are in a unique time of development. Their hormones are getting stabilized, their tailbones are forming, and their attention spans are limited. Simply put, middle grades students need to move. Not constantly. But yes, some movement during a class period is conducive to learning. Keep this in mind the next time you are forced to sit in a six-hour professional development session and listen to a speaker. If you find that difficult as an adult, then how much more challenging is it for your students?

There are many benefits to young adolescents if they are allowed to move while learning. Movement

- Gives their brains time to rejuvenate.

- Gives their brains time to consolidate new information.

- Improves discipline.

- Improves student motivation.

- Wakes up their bodies as they begin to tire.

- Increases blood circulation.

- Moves more oxygen to the brain.

- Creates a social environment.

- Creates an exciting environment.

- Creates a fun environment (Allen, 2008; Lengel & Kuczala, 2010).

When we talk about allowing students to move around the classroom, some teachers get nervous because they imagine the classroom management issues that will ensue. Yes, classroom management can be an issue, but that can be resolved with solid and consistent procedures (see Chapter 12). However, it is much easier to get most students to behave appropriately and on-task if they are enjoying what they are doing. Some classroom management issues are simply a result of bored students becoming disengaged and being tired of sitting still for hours on end. Kim Campbell (2014) maintains that it may be counterintuitive, but getting students moving actually improves students' behavior. However, she recommends teachers set four ground rules to follow in planning for an activity that incorporates movement. Carefully thinking through each of these before the lesson begins can prevent a multitude of issues:

1. Be purposeful in how you move your students.

2. Anticipate the challenges.

3. Plan how to direct your students back to you and to the lesson.

4. Have a back-up plan if the activity fails to meet your expectations (Campbell, 2014, p. 12-13).

Kellough and Kellough (1978) describe a framework to consider that relates directly to physically active learning. The Learning Experiences Ladder strengthens student learning by getting them as close to the top of the ladder as possible in any learning experience. The closer a learning experience is to a direct experience, the better the quality of learning.

Verbal Experiences—Teacher talk, written words, abstract symbolization, students physically inactive

Visual Experiences—Still pictures, diagrams, charts, students physically inactive

Vicarious Experiences—Computer programs, video programs, learner indirectly "doing", some limited physical activity

Simulated Experiences—Role-playing, experimenting, simulations, working models, closest to the real thing, students physically engaged

Direct Experiences—Learner actually doing what is being learned, true inquiry, usually integrates multiple disciplines

This chapter is full of generic activities that allow for physical movement in the classroom. Any of these strategies can be used to teach different content in various subject areas. Be flexible with the strategies and adapt them to suit your purposes and your style. The point of all of these activities is to allow students the opportunity to get out of their seats, to shake off a little of the boredom, and to get more engaged with the content.

Scrambled Eggs

This idea comes from Patra Griffitt in Harlem, Georgia, and can transform any worksheet into a physically active learning experience. All you need is a collection of plastic Easter eggs, a marker, and scissors to cut up a worksheet.

To prepare the activity, number each egg on the outside with the marker. Next, cut up the worksheet so each question, problem, or item is on a separate slip of paper. Place the items in the eggs so the number of each worksheet item is in the corresponding egg. Arrange the students into partners. When it is time to begin the activity, each set of partners has one runner go to the table in front of the room, select one of the eggs, and bring the egg back to their desk to open. Once the students have opened their eggs, the partners work together to determine the answer and record it on their answer sheet. Next, the other partner runs to the front, replaces the first egg, and selects a different one. They can do the eggs in any order. When time is called, the class goes over the answers and the students check their papers with a different colored pen, correcting the incorrect answers as they go.

Practical Suggestions

- An important rule is that the runner must be seated before opening the egg, otherwise you will have pieces of eggs and slips of paper flying everywhere.

- Have two or three sets of identical eggs in two or three different trays. Because there will be multiple eggs with the same number, if a group gets stuck on one question, then other groups will have access to the same problem or question through one of the other sets.

- Save your numbered eggs. This activity can easily be reused with another worksheet later in the year.

- You may want to have a prize for the team with the most answers correct.

Matching Plates

This activity is perfect for things that come in pairs, such as a vocabulary term and its definition, a problem and its answer, an event and its date, a country and its leader, or a question and its answer. For this activity you will need some cheap paper plates (one for each student) and two markers of different colors. Write questions or vocabulary terms on one half of the plates using one of the markers. Write the answers or definitions on the second half of the plates using a different colored marker. Each plate should have exactly one plate that corresponds with it.

Distribute the plates randomly to the students and then tell them to find their matches. If students are holding questions, then students who have the answers to their questions are their matches. If students are holding vocabulary terms, then the students who have their definitions are their matches. Once the students have found their matches, they stand back-to-back and hold up their plates. When all of the students in the class have found their matches, have the students who have the answers turn their plates facing their chests. The students who have the questions keep their plates facing out. Have the students read their questions one at a time and then have the rest of the class answer the question. The student with the plate containing the correct answer will inform the class if they were correct or not.

Practical Suggestions

- It is possible to appear that you are randomly handing out plates, when in fact, you are strategically handing plates of one color to higher-functioning students and plates of the other color to lower-functioning students. This will ensure that you have heterogeneous groups if you want the students who match to be partners in the next activity.

- Allow the students to help each other determine their matches and to refer to their textbooks or notes.

Task Cards

A task card is simply a card that has one task on it. It could be a question, a math problem, a sentence to diagram, or any small task. Although a set of task cards is equivalent to one worksheet, task cards have more flexibility and utility. Get your students physically active by placing task cards around the room and have them move to the different cards to answer or solve them. To add differentiation to the activity, the teacher sends some students to more challenging task cards and other students to cards covering the regular content. The number of games that can be created using task cards is limited only by your imagination. Although sets of task cards are available for online purchase, teachers can make them by simply cutting up a worksheet, pasting the items on different cards, and laminating them. Place them around the room, set some rules and structure, and let students move.

- Color code the cards by gluing the cards to colored paper to make differentiation easier. Different students can be assigned to do different-colored cards.

- To eliminate using copy paper for worksheets, laminate the cards so they can be reused by multiple classes and reused next year.

Snowball Fight

Who doesn't like a good snowball fight? This activity is a perfect way to enliven a class and transform a worksheet or workbook page into a lot of fun. First, either provide a sheet of paper for each student or have them provide a sheet of their own. Write one question or problem on each sheet of paper. Open-ended questions that have multiple answers or ideas work best. Distribute the papers to the students and ask them to answer the question on their piece of paper. If it is a math problem, you might ask them to complete the first step. If it is an open-ended question, have them write just one idea in a sentence. Once students have written their responses, the teacher asks everyone to crumple up their paper and throw it in the air. Each student picks up a new "snowball" from the floor. They then respond to or add to what the person before them wrote. The process repeats. When the teacher decides the snowball fight should end, the teacher leads a whole class discussion, asking students to share ideas or answers from their snowballs (Harris, 2011).

Practical Suggestions

- Enforce the rule that each snowball is thrown only once when you give them the go ahead.

- You may choose for every paper to be a different question or problem, or you may choose for some questions or problems to be repeated on more than one sheet of paper. This is easily done on a computer.

- Asking students to share something from their papers takes pressure off of the student because the student is sharing something a classmate said and not necessarily his or her own idea. This works great for getting students to participate who are normally reluctant to share their own thoughts.

Popcorn

In this activity, arrange students in partners with one partner designated the "kernel" and one partner designated the "popcorn". The teacher poses a question and determines a period of time for the kernels to share their thoughts while the popcorns listen. Next, at the teacher's signal the roles are reversed as the popcorns share their thoughts while their kernel partners listen. At this point, the teacher signals for the popcorn to pop. When the signal is given, the students who are designated as popcorn, move about the room to find a different partner while the kernels remain seated. The process repeats (Udvari-Solner & Kluth, 2008).

Practical Suggestions

- Display on the board a timer such as online-stopwatch. com to help keep students focused.

- To avoid having to yell increasingly louder to get students' attention, have a signal to get your students' attention at each point in the activity.

Four Corners

Four corners is a good strategy for questions that are divergent and have more than one possible answer and it also works well for opinion questions. It requires students to get out of their seats and move while taking a stand on an issue. Write each of the words *agree, strongly agree, disagree,* and *strongly disagree* (or write *A, B, C,* and *D*) in bold letters on different sheets of poster paper (one word or letter per poster). Tape one poster to each corner of the room.

The teacher reads and posts on the board a statement for students to consider. Students decide if they agree, disagree, strongly agree, or strongly disagree. If using the A–D posters, the teacher poses a multiple-choice question, and the students decide whether A, B, C, or D is the correct answer. After giving students a few moments to decide which corner they believe is the best one, the teacher asks the students to move to that corner. The students pair off with another student in their corner to discuss their position. The teacher leads a class discussion by asking students from different corners to discuss their positions and to convince students in other corners that they are correct.

Practical Suggestions

- Sometimes an issue, question, or problem may indicate using only two corners. For example, "Move to the corner in the front by the bookcase if you believe the answer is positive, and move to the corner in the back by the file cabinet if you believe the answer is negative".

- For repeated use, laminate your posters.

Give One, Get One

This strategy (Kagan & Kagan, 2009) offers the benefit of getting students physically moving around the classroom while challenging them to share ideas with multiple classmates, not just their best friends.

Write a high-level, open-ended question that has multiple answers about the content students are learning and post the question on the board. Next, students write their ideas based on the text or what they know. Then the students circulate around the room, and each student shares one idea with someone and collects an idea from the same person. Then the student goes to a different person and repeats the process of "Give one idea and get one idea." A student may not collect more than one idea from any one person. If a student finds a person with the same idea, the two students must work together to come up with a new idea. Each student must collect four new ideas.

Once all the students have their collections of ideas, the teacher begins the whole class discussion by asking students to share ideas from their lists. The whole class discussion allows the class to compile a master list of the key ideas that were important in the chapter or unit.

Practical Suggestions

- Using a timer helps students remain focused and on task. If they know there is a time limit, they will be less likely to wander.

- Asking students to share an idea from their papers takes pressure off of students because they are sharing something a group member said and not necessarily a personal idea. This is effective in getting participation from students who are normally reluctant to share their own thoughts.

Scavenger Hunt

A great way to reinforce vocabulary, the scavenger hunt requires students to find examples of various terms. Teachers might ask students to find examples of geometric figures, such as, "find a set of alternate interior angles in the classroom" or "find two similar but not congruent equilateral triangles in the classroom" and then have students take pictures of each item they find on their list. Or you might have students cut examples out of newspapers or magazines, such as "find a compound sentence" or "find a sentence written in passive voice."

Create a list of things for your students to find related to your content objective. Distribute the list to the students and allow them to refer to their notes or textbooks if they are unsure of any definitions of vocabulary terms found on the list. Allow the students to move about the room to find as many items on the list as they can. When time is called, determine which group has the most items and allow the rest of the class to judge whether or not they have correctly identified the items they found.

Practical Suggestions

- Relax and have a little fun—it is okay if the classroom gets a little messy.

- If students take photos, they could use various phone or tablet apps such as Skitch to label their pictures or to label particular aspects of a picture.

Airplane Questions

This strategy (Edwards, 2014) allows students to move in the classroom, while also demonstrating their well-honed paper airplane making skills. As students arrive in the classroom, give each student a sheet with a question or problem on it and ask them to make a paper airplane, but tell them not to answer the question. One at a time, ask students to come to the front of the room and throw their airplanes. The student closest to where the airplane lands is the first to respond to the question. The teacher then allows other students to help or add to the first student's response.

Practical Suggestions

- Because students can spend quite a bit of class time folding a plane, this strategy will likely get infrequent use. It can be a nice diversion from a monotonous day.

- Put a separate question on each sheet or repeat some questions on multiple sheets.

- Ratchet up the fun by offering a prize for the plane that flies the farthest or the plane that has the most creative flight plan.

Learning Stations

Using learning stations is a perfect strategy for middle grades classrooms for several reasons including the fact that they get students out of their seats while learning. Learning stations allow students to do hands-on activities in small groups and allow the groups to rotate through a variety of activities, thus bringing in multiple learning approaches. They are also a way to structure differentiation so a group of students can work only on activities at their level, while a different group of students is working on activities at a different level. Learning stations are designated places with variously-structured activities around the classroom that students rotate through. Examples of stations:

- Computers or tablets where students engage in a technology activity

- A table with the teacher giving small group instruction based on the needs of students in that group

- A game that gives students practice in a particular skill

- An exploratory activity

The stations can include whatever activities you wish for students to complete. Each station should be self-explanatory with written directions for students and all the needed materials. The activities should be tasks that students can complete independently or in small groups with little or no guidance.

Practical Suggestions

- Learning stations are a good method for differentiation, because the students can be grouped according to formative assessment data and can complete tasks at different levels.

- Quickly review the directions for each station before sending students to them to make sure they understand what is expected of them.

- Have a clear signal that lets students know when it is time to move to the next station.

Interactive Board

Many classrooms are now equipped with interactive boards that allow the teacher to manipulate objects projected from the computer. Allowing students to interact at the board incorporates physical activity into the classroom.

Create an interactive template that matches your content objective. Your interactive board likely has a set of these already prepared and many can be found online and easily downloaded. Once you have displayed the template on the board, simply let students come to the board one-at-a-time and manipulate the objects or information. Another option is to use the interactive board as a station while doing learning stations. This allows a small group of students to work on the interactive board while at that station.

Practical Suggestions

- While students go to the interactive board one-at-a-time to manipulate pieces of information, students at their seats can quietly replicate what is on the board in their notes.

- When a student goes to the board, they can either move a piece of information that has not been previously placed or they can correct a piece of information that a previous classmate had placed.

Beach Ball

This is a fun activity that adds energy to the class and gets every student involved. Using a marker, write items related to the content objective randomly across an inflatable plastic beach ball. These items could be math problems, vocabulary terms, or numbers corresponding to questions in the textbook or workbook.

The teacher throws the ball to a student. The student catches the ball, answering whatever item his or her right index finger is pointing to. If the student answers the question correctly the student can sit down. If the student answers the question incorrectly, the student remains standing and throws the ball to another student who must answer the same question. Play continues until everyone is seated.

Practical Suggestions

- Increase the challenge by requiring students to give examples of vocabulary terms or explain how they know their answer to the math problem was correct.

- Using a dry-erase marker allows the teacher to clean the ball and put different items on it for the next activity.

Role Playing and Drama

This strategy allows the content to come alive in your classroom while encouraging both creativity and movement on the part of your students.

Print scenarios directly related to a content objective for students to act out by role-playing or give them topics upon which to base the writing of their own drama. Assign different scenarios to different groups of students. Students need less time for planning a role-playing activity than for writing a drama. Students perform the role-plays at the front of the room and one group at a time. The rest of the class determines which events groups are enacting. Role-playing and drama bring energy and creativity into the classroom in a way that is different from other instructional methods. Rich Allen underscores this in his statement, "All the world's a stage—especially the classroom" (Allen, 2008, p. 131).

Practical Suggestion

- Display a timer at the front of the room, so that students can see how much time they have left to plan their scene. Middle grades students will take as much time as you let them, so be aware of saving some precious class time for discussion and reflection on the content enacted.

Stand Up, Sit Down

This is a simple, easy strategy that teachers can incorporate into any lesson with basically no preparation. In Stand Up, Sit Down the teacher poses a question related to the content objective. Students stand up if they agree and sit down if they disagree (or vice versa). There are unlimited possibilities for question types to use in this activity. For example: true/false questions; write two possible answers to a question on the board and ask students to stand up if they think it is the first answer and sit down if they think it is the second answer.

Practical Suggestion

- After posing the question, give the students a few moments to think before asking them to stand up or sit down.

Let 4 Come to the Board

This activity allows movement during guided practice. The teacher assigns students a task to do, which could be a question from the book, a math problem, a sentence to diagram, or any other task. While students are working on the task at their desks, the teacher selects four students (or more if there is space) to work the task on the board. Since all students in the class are doing the task at the same time, no one is really paying attention to how anyone else is solving it (but they could if they get stuck). When students have had sufficient time to complete the task, the teacher asks students about their solution or answer, perhaps comparing and contrasting different solutions that students have written on the board.

Practical Suggestions

- Feel free to help the students at the board, just as you would help the students at their seats.

- Be sure to call on different students to work on the board for each new task.

Building Models and Dioramas

This strategy allows students to create a physical representation of a concept, event, or phenomenon that they are studying. It not only gives students the opportunity to move and to learn in a hands-on manner, but it also gives them the opportunity to be creative.

Prepare an assignment sheet that explains to students what information must be represented and how their models will be evaluated. Collect whatever materials students will need to build their models. Explain to students what information you want presented and how they will be evaluated. Give students as much freedom to be creative as you can, but provide some parameters that ensure they will learn the content.

Practical Suggestion

- Give students short deadlines. For example, "You must have a sketch of what you are going to build completed by 11:15 a.m."

Whip Around

Students stand up in pairs back-to-back. The teacher poses a question or a problem for the students to solve. Each student writes a response on an individual dry-erase board. When the teacher says, "Whip Around!" the students turn and compare their answers to their partners' response. They then discuss the question or problem and resolve any differences before the teacher leads a class in a discussion of the question or problem (Harris, 2011).

Practical Suggestions

- If you do not have student dry-erase boards, paper and a clipboard will work just fine.

- To differentiate, simply give different pairs of students different questions. Just make sure that students who are paired together have the same question.

Circle Activity

This idea comes from Tanya McLain, a language arts teacher in Evans, Georgia. Tanya combined the games hot potato and musical chairs into an instructional review activity. The students stand in a circle around the room and toss a squishy ball around the circle while music is playing. When the music stops, whoever is holding the squishy ball has to answer the question posed by the teacher. As the students answer questions they sit down and the circle gets smaller and smaller.

Practical Suggestions

- Having more than one circle in the classroom allows more students to answer questions at one time and therefore, increases participation opportunities.

- Have the question displayed on the board while the music is playing so that students have time to think about the question as they are tossing the ball.

- Tanya added some motivation by requiring the student who answers the question correctly to say, "I'm a smartie" and she gave them a roll of Smarties™.

Manipulatives

Educators have long accepted manipulatives as an effective strategy for kinesthetic learners because they give students the opportunity to move somewhat while they are learning and help them move from concrete to visual to abstract representations of concepts.

The implementation varies depending on the concept and the manipulative. In general, a discovery-type approach is better than a teacher-directed approach. If not done correctly, manipulatives can just turn an activity into a procedural, follow-the-teacher, step-by-step activity in which students simply copy teacher procedures—which is no different than copying procedures with pencil and paper. The value of manipulatives is that they give students a deep understanding as they see the concept acted out visually and in a hands-on manner.

Practical Suggestion

• Sort the manipulatives into small containers or baggies making it easy to distribute to groups or individual students during class.

Lab Experiments

Lab experiments are another way of incorporating physical movement into your classroom. There are numerous experiments that can be used to teach almost any concept in science. An experiment will help students better understand a concept and allow them to move as well.

Practical Suggestion

• In a classroom without lab tables, use an arrangement of tables around the perimeter of the classroom. Having designated stations at which groups of students perform experiments requires them to get up out of their normal desks and stand.

Carousel

This strategy (Spencer, 2008) is a perfect choice for open-ended questions related to the unit you are studying. It allows the students to move around the room and forces them to consider multiple ideas for each question. Write open-ended questions related to the concept you are teaching on sheets of chart paper and place them around the room. You will need as many pieces of chart paper as the number of groups. Each chart paper will have a different question written on it.

Assign the students to small groups and give each group a different colored marker. Each group rotates through the chart papers and makes a different comment or gives a different answer than the groups before them. This continues until every group has responded to the question on every sheet of chart paper.

Practical Suggestions

- It is fine to have more pieces of chart paper than the number of groups.

- Use a timer to determine when the groups switch to the next chart.

Podium in the Back of the Room

This is a good strategy for the particularly restless student who wants to move constantly. Place a podium or have some other designated spot in the back of the room. If a student feels the need to move around when it is not an appropriate time in the lesson to do so, the student is allowed to stand at the podium. While standing at the podium, the student must continue doing whatever the class is doing. The student is not allowed to distract other students while at the podium, but can move around as long as he is touching the podium.

Practical Suggestions

- Do not make the podium a punitive thing. It is simply an alternative if a student wants to move around or stretch.

- If a student abuses the podium option or distracts other students, the teacher may use the veto power of the teacher to remove the privilege.

Kick Me

This strategy (Macauley, 2014) is a variation of the old prank where someone puts a "kick me" sign on another person's back. But in this case, the sign on the back is a vocabulary term. Every student has a word on his or her back. All students have a sheet with a list of definitions, and they circulate looking at everyone's back and filling in the blanks on the sheet with the information they glean. Another option is for the words on students' backs to be answers to fill-in-the-blank questions, and still another option is to have the signs be answers to math problems.

Practical Suggestion

- Using a timer helps students remain focused and on task. If they know there is a time limit, they will be less likely to wander.

Conclusion

As with every active learning strategy, physical activity in the classroom should be purposeful. The goal is neither movement for movement's sake nor having fun. Be sure that when you plan physically active strategies in your lessons the physical movement enhances the learning of the concepts rather than distracts students from learning those concepts. Strategically incorporating some opportunities for physical movement in your classroom can greatly enhance the motivation and cooperation of students.

Part Two

Introduction
Practical Classroom Strategies

In Part 1 we talked about multiple strategies that get students intellectually, socially, and physically active in the classroom. Now, we will turn our attention to strategies that are effective for getting students engaged and also intersect with one or more of the three dimensions in the Active Learning Framework. These strategies can be used across content areas to teach a wide-range of topics and have the potential to get students motivated and engaged in the content.

Chapter 5 is an acknowledgement that lectures are here to stay, but they do not have to be boring. This chapter has numerous ideas for getting middle grades students actively involved as they interact with content during lectures. Chapter 6 provides excellent games to get students actively learning while having fun. Finally, Chapter 7 makes it easy for teachers to connect middle grades digital natives to content.

As we discuss these strategies that involve active learning, we will indicate where they intersect with the three dimensions of the Active Learning Framework. Often, the intersection depends on the implementation. For example, the kinds of questions a teacher asks during a game determines whether or not it involves intellectually active learning. Whether students play a game in teams or individually determines if it involves socially active learning. It is the teacher's role to determine the amount of active learning that occurs when using these practical classroom strategies.

Chapter 5

Interactive Lectures

The secret of being a bore is to tell everything.
~Voltaire

This chapter acknowledges that PowerPoint is here to stay and that teachers commonly lecture in middle grades classrooms. Therefore, this chapter focuses on how to spice up those lectures to engage students rather than expect them to passively listen (or pretend to listen). Although I strongly advocate that teachers incorporate active learning, I do not suggest throwing direct instruction completely out the window. There is still a time, place, and necessity for direct instruction. As Meyers and Jones (1993) suggest,

> What we need to remember is that the choice between lecture and active learning is not simply a case of either-or. Usually the problem is not a little reliance on lecture, but too much of it. (p. 14)

Hopefully, you will consider using fewer lectures. When you do lecture, make it brief.

Students will engage more if lectures are punctuated with short, interactive strategies that let students share in the work of teaching and learning (Meyers & Jones, 1993). In terms of lectures, two things help middle grades students experience success. First, a lecture, just like any other activity, should not last longer than 10–15 minutes. If it goes longer, students' attention wanes. Even if they are still sitting quietly, their attention is declining. Second, the teacher should break up the lecture with short activities requiring students to interact with the teacher and the content. The following strategies fit in after every 2–3 slides of a PowerPoint. Teachers of any content areas can use any of these strategies, adapting them to suit various purposes and styles. These strategies fall in different areas on the active learning framework: intellectual, social, and physical.

Pose a Question

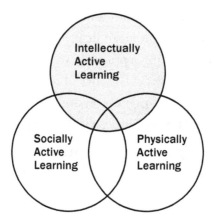

This may seem obvious, but it is an often overlooked strategy. First, the teacher covers a couple slides' worth of information and then pauses. The next slide is a question directly related to the material just covered. After reviewing their notes, all the students provide their answers. The higher the level of the question on Bloom's Taxonomy, the better. The teacher reteaches depending on the number and types of wrong answers. If students provide a consistent wrong answer, the teacher clarifies that particular misunderstanding. Several methods allow teachers to quickly and easily get an answer from every student and to discern which students understood the covered material. When asking the question, the teacher gives students an appropriate amount of time to review their notes and then asks everyone to submit their answer simultaneously. This prevents students from waiting to see what the most popular answer is before submitting a response and provides more accurate formative assessment data.

- Clickers—Student response systems allow students to electronically submit an answer, which the computer tabulates. The computer can calculate the number for each response of a multiple-choice question and can provide a report of the answer for each individual student if students received assigned clickers that were tracked.

- Plickers—This is a more economical version of clickers. Plickers.com provides free printable cards that can be scanned by tablet or smartphone. The students hold up their cards and turn it so their answer choice is facing up. Scanning all of the cards, the teacher quickly gets a report of how many students answered each response choice.

- Number Fans—Number fans are the economical, low-tech version of clickers. Each student gets a ring with the digits 0–9 printed on individual strips of cardstock and laminated. The students hold up their choices of the correct answer. If it is a multiple-choice question, they hold up 1 if they think the answer is A, 2 if they think the answer is B, and so on. For math problems, they hold up the number they think is the correct answer, such as 57.

- Student Boards—If students have individual small, dry-erase boards, they write their answer and hold it up for the teacher to see. Student boards are particularly suited to writing answers to open-ended or short answer questions in addition to multiple-choice and true/false.

- Padlet—Padlet.com provides another method of collecting answers to open-ended or short-answer questions. If students have their own device that is connected to the Internet, they can sign into the digital wall the teacher created and post their response. The teacher is able to display all of the responses made by students simultaneously on the same wall.

- Poll Everywhere—This website allows students to text an answer to the teacher by using their phones to select an answer from choices provided or to type in a constructed response. The teacher can display the responses for the entire class to see.

Game

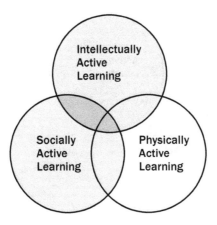

This strategy is basically the same as the last one, with a twist of fun and excitement. The class plays an ongoing game that lasts throughout the lecture. The teacher covers 2 or 3 slides of information and then switches to a game (see Chapter 6 for ideas). Every 2 or 3 slides, the class plays one round of the game based on the information just covered. The teacher divides the class into two teams and each team gets to answer one question. Then the teacher goes back to the lecture, covers a couple more slides, returns to the game for another round, and so on. Points accumulate throughout the lecture and the game ends when the lecture ends.

Guess What's Next

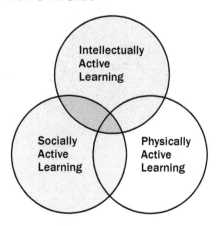

Guessing can be motivating and can get students intrigued about what the teacher is preparing to share. The teacher creates a slide with two pictures related to the content of the next informational slide (new information to the class). The teacher poses a question and asks the students to mentally guess (not out loud) whether they think the answer will be picture A or picture B. Here are the steps to the strategy:

- Students think individually and guess silently in their heads.

- Students pair up with a neighbor and discuss their individual guesses.

- Students have to commit to an answer in their mind.

- The teacher takes a vote and students raise their hands guessing either A or B.

- The teacher moves to the next slide and gives the answer along with whatever information explains the correct response.

Partner Up

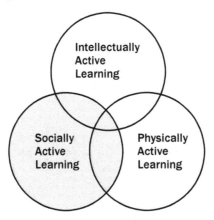

This is a quick and easy way to get students interacting with the content and literally requires no preparation. After introducing 2 or 3 slides' worth of information, the teacher tells students to partner up. Have each set of partners agree on which person is partner A and which person is partner B. After setting a timer, the teacher asks partner A to review everything that was said so far for 30 seconds. When the timer sounds, partner B says everything that A did not say for 20 seconds.

Pause Procedure

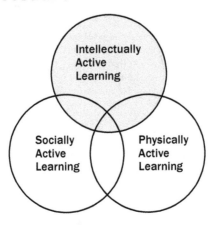

Ruhl, Hughes, and Schloss (1987) found in their research study that students will learn more information if the teacher pauses for a couple minutes during a lecture and allows students to consolidate their notes. When giving students a couple minutes to go back and make sense of their notes teachers can remind them to use highlighters or draw a quick concept map outlining the key points. Perhaps they can elaborate or add more detail. The idea is for students to have time to make sense of what they wrote. Until middle grades students have practiced and are familiar with this strategy, teachers have to add more structure or give them specific directions such as, "Make a table of the actions and results we just discussed".

Three-Minute Review

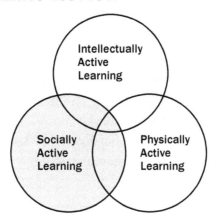

This strategy (Moore, 2009) is somewhat similar to the Partner Up strategy. Before starting the lecture, the teacher directs students to get into small groups. After a few slides of the lecture, students discuss the ideas just presented, review the concepts, and ask each other questions (if they have them) about what they just learned. The group time should be approximately three minutes, after which the process continues with a few more slides of lecture followed by more group time.

Conclusion

The purpose of all of these strategies is to increase student engagement with the content. Realistically, middle grades students will not retain as much information if they are passively listening to a lecture for a long period of time. Students are more likely to retain information if these interactive strategies are peppered throughout a 10- to 15-minute lecture. The strategies shared in this chapter are an attempt to acknowledge direct instruction as an appropriate method if it includes active participation of middle grades students. Many educators take an extreme either–or approach: either you are doing direct instruction or you are doing active learning. Those two ideas do not have to be mutually exclusive; it is possible to get students engaged actively while they receive direct instruction.

Chapter 6
Games

In teaching the greatest sin is to be boring.
~J. F. Herbart

What middle grades student doesn't love a good game? The energy and level of engagement in the classroom ramps up quickly when students play a game. Using a variety of instructional approaches is important, and games are a valuable tool for occasional use. Games transform the passive student into an active participant in the learning process, and they remind both the student and the teacher that energy in the classroom is a good thing. Not about having a good time, but about learning the content, every game, just like every other active learning strategy, must be purposeful and aligned with your content objectives. This is real learning and not fluff.

A quick Internet search of any content area provides numerous games in a variety of formats that enhance student learning. There are practice-type games that review information already learned, digital games, low-tech games, and inquiry-type games in which students learn content knowledge as they play.

An instructional game could fall anywhere on the active learning framework. Let's take a tried and true favorite game of middle grades students, trashketball. In trashketball, when students answer a question correctly, they shoot a trashball into the trash can. If they are successful, they earn points. Now let's think about how to align this game with the Active Learning Framework.

Physically Active

This game automatically incorporates physical activity because students get to get out of their seats and throw the trashball. Ideally, every student will have that opportunity. At its bare bones, the game falls in the physically active dimension on the framework.

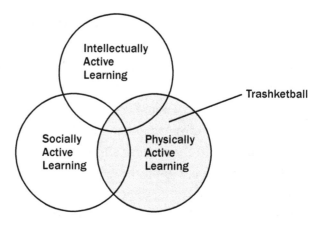

Socially Active

Socially active learning can be incorporated by structuring a strategy so that students work in teams to play the game. After teams have had sufficient time to discuss the question or problem, the teacher randomly calls on a team to answer the question. If that team answers correctly, the team sends a representative to shoot the trashball for the team. If the students work together in teams to answer the questions, the game intersects with the socially active dimension:

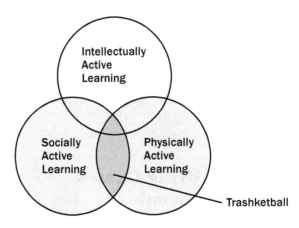

Intellectually Active

Increasing the challenge of the questions incorporates intellectually active learning into the game. If students answer recall and comprehension level questions, then the game remains outside of the intellectually active circle. However, if the questions move up Bloom's Taxonomy to analysis, application, synthesis, and evaluate types of questions, then the game would intersect with all three types of learning on the active learning framework:

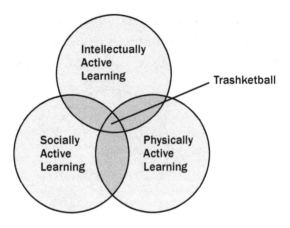

Intellectually
Active
Learning

Trashketball

Socially
Active
Learning

Physically
Active
Learning

Benefits of Using Games in the Classroom

Increase in Student Engagement

Upon announcement of a game in a lesson, the teacher can literally see a complete transformation in the level of energy and engagement in a group of students. Previously apathetic students all of a sudden will start digging in and trying to get all the correct answers. Games motivate students to interact with the content, maintain student interest, and increase participation. Games draw on young adolescents' natural competitive instincts. Another advantage of games is that they are disarming; students are drawn into learning before they have time to let their normal reservations about learning kick in. Today's teachers are competing with smartphones, tablets, and video gaming systems, and games can level the playing field as they make learning fun and bring laughter into a lesson (Udvari-Solner & Kluth, 2008). Games provide intrinsic rewards, which are extremely helpful in motivating young adolescents.

Cooperation and Teamwork

Games also contribute to better peer relationships and a positive classroom atmosphere. Particularly in team games students must be able to cooperate and get along with their peers to win. Games are helpful in building cooperation and teamwork skills that young adolescents need to be successful in life. Teamwork and the ability to collaborate are qualities that employers consistently say they are looking for in employees (Hansen & Hansen, 2010).

Assessment

Games are a form of assessment. Playing a game can enable students to self-assess what they understand and what they need to work on. Games provide immediate feedback on their performance. That feedback can be helpful to students as it allows them to gauge their understanding and improve that understanding without the stress and consequences of grades. Using games as a formative assessment tool, teachers can observe what misunderstandings and difficulties their students are having and adjust their instruction accordingly.

Challenge

Games by nature have inherent challenge built in but can make tackling the challenge fun. Difficult questions are less threatening because they are just part of the game, and instinctively the players know that a game is supposed to have challenge built in so it will be interesting. Games can encourage students to try even the most difficult content in a fun, lighthearted way. Games can help students take risks in front of their peers ("it's just a game"), which is something they normally avoid doing (Udvari-Solner & Kluth, 2008).

Games also reinforce strategic thinking skills because students have to make decisions as they navigate through the structure of a game. The beauty of a game is that students can gain immediate satisfaction and accomplishment if they are successful with the difficult content they have experienced during the game.

How to Use Games

After reviewing numerous action research studies, Marzano (2010) concludes that games can increase student achievement by 20 percentile points if used correctly. What are important considerations in order to ensure student learning during games?

Be Purposeful

Begin with your learning objective. What is it that you want your students to learn? It is critical to keep the answer to this question in the center of your focus as you select or design your game. If you lose this focus, it might be tempting to just have some fun in the middle of class at the risk of the learning being lost. It should not be possible for a student who has no understanding of your learning objective to win your game. Knowing the content must be a requirement for getting points in any game. Target essential content in every question that students must answer to earn points. By keeping this simple rule in mind, you will ensure that your students are learning or reinforcing their learning while having a good time.

Require Explanations

Another important method for ensuring that learning is happening during the game is to require explanations or evidence for answers. In other words, just answering the question correctly is not enough to score a point. Students must give some explanation or evidence to back up the answer. If a team misses a question, other teams must identify and explain how that team's error can be corrected before scoring their points. It should not be possible for students to just guess an answer choice and earn points for a lucky guess.

Debriefing after the game extends the learning. The teacher can emphasize certain concepts that confused students during the game. The teacher can also create a question similar to one that students missed during the game to ensure the class has understood the concept.

Revise Notes as You Play

Marzano (2010) recommends that you give students time to revise their notes during or after a game. Students may have important details or nuances to the content to add to their notes. As with any active learning strategy, there should always be opportunities for students to revise their understanding of the concepts. The tally of the final score should not be the end of learning.

Play for Fun

Another recommendation by Marzano (2010) is to keep the game low-stakes and inconsequential. There should be some lighthearted reward for the winning team; however, you want to keep the team scores away from the grade book. Students will enjoy friendly competition as long as the stakes are not high. The points and rewards are simply for fun.

Also, be sure to rearrange your students into different teams throughout the year so everyone gets to experience winning. Nothing stifles motivation quicker than always being on the losing team.

Keep the Challenge High

Finally, design the game so it is challenging, but not frustrating. You want to build in opportunities for success and positive reinforcement. Keep Vygotsky's Zone of Proximal Development (ZPD) in mind. The ZPD is the area between what students can do with support and what they can do independently (Vygotsky, 1962). Not every question in the game should be below your students' ZPD; that would make the game too easy and no fun. People inherently like to be challenged. On the other hand, the game would not be fun if it is so hard that it is beyond your students' ZPD. Since every class has a range of student ability, it is often helpful to include questions that range in difficulty. An easy question can allow students with lower ability levels to experience success. When a difficult question comes along, students with higher ability levels can appreciate the challenge.

Games as Stations

Games do not always have to be played with the whole class. Teachers can incorporate games into learning stations and use them as a differentiation tool. Many games available in different content areas can be played either in a small group or with partners. A small group could play a game at one station, while other students are doing other activities. As students finish up seatwork, they could get folder games from a box in the corner of the classroom. The directions for these games are included in the folders, are easy to figure out, and are doable with a partner. With some creativity, teachers can find many different ways to structure and incorporate games into their classrooms.

Examples of Games

Following are some generic games that teachers can use to teach different content in various subject areas. The games are flexible and adaptable to suit different purposes and styles.

Dry-Erase Tray Hockey

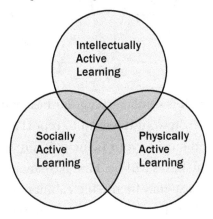

The game is a simple concept. Once a team answers a question correctly (providing a good explanation, of course), they get to send a representative to the dry-erase board. The player uses the dry-erase marker as the "hockey stick" and the eraser as the "hockey puck". The teacher draws lines that are evenly spaced on the board. The first line represents the starting position. The other lines represent increasing point values, and the team scores points based on how far they slide the "hockey puck" (eraser) down the tray before it falls off the tray and onto the floor. For example, if the lines each represent 10 points and the player gets it past the first two lines before it falls off the tray, then the team earns 20 points.

Classroom Baseball

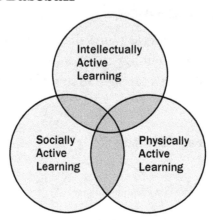

Classroom baseball is similar to regular baseball, just without the bat and ball (you wouldn't want to report a broken window or Smartboard to your principal). First, the teacher decides where the bases will be. First base may be the middle window, second base may be the file cabinet in the back of the room, etc. After the teacher divides the class into two teams, the first team sends their first "batter" to the front of the room, which is home plate. The teacher asks a question, and if the batter answers it correctly, the batter moves to first base. Just like in regular baseball, the team keeps sending batters until they miss a question. As each batter gets a question correct, the players who are already on base get to advance to the next base until someone makes a run to score a point. To keep the game moving, allow only one strike per team. Once the first team makes an out, the second team bats. The teacher decides the number of innings to play, and of course, the team with the highest score at the bottom of the last inning wins.

To differentiate, vary the levels of difficulty of the questions: singles are the easiest questions, doubles are a little more difficult, triples are more difficult, and homeruns are the most challenging. The teacher can let the batter select which type of hit he or she wants to try to make.

Balloon Race

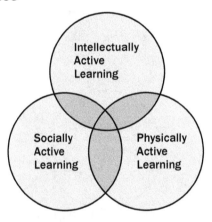

This is a high energy game and lots of fun. After the teacher divides the class into teams, one representative from each team comes to their team's designated section of the board and faces the class. The teacher asks a question, the students write the correct answer on the board behind them, and then the students run to their team's designated chair and sit on the balloon in that chair. The first team to have the correct answer on the board and to pop their balloon gets the point.

Pictionary

This is a simple game that does not require a lot of preparation. The teacher makes a list of vocabulary terms, events, concepts, etc. and puts them on slips of paper. A student comes to the front of the room and draws a slip of paper. Just as in the real game Pictionary® sold by Hasbro, the player must get his or her team to guess the concept or the word by drawing pictures on the board before the timer goes off. Before the game begins, the teacher establishes rules such as the players at the board cannot write letters or numbers and cannot say anything.

Password

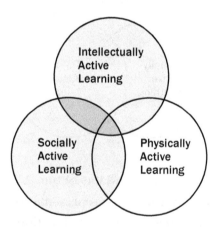

While this game was on television way before your students' time (and possibly yours as well), it is an oldie but goodie. The teacher divides the class into teams. One person from Team 1 comes to the front of the room and sits at a desk that faces the rest of the class. The student's back is to the board, where the teacher displays a vocabulary term. The rest of the team tries to get the student to guess the word behind them within the time limit, which should be about 30 seconds. The clues should relate to the definition of the word or examples of the term, but the one rule is that they cannot say any part of the word on the board. If the student correctly guesses the word, the team gets a point. The teams alternate turns and every round a different student comes to the board. The advantage of this game is that students have to put definitions into their own words and think about the real meanings of terms as well as examples.

Bingo

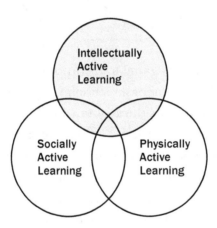

Every student gets a blank Bingo board. The teacher displays a list of answers on the board. The students write those answers in random order on their sheet. A blank Bingo board will have 24 empty squares, so you will need to display at least 24 answers. But you can put more than 24. Next, the teacher randomly draws one of the questions that belongs to one of the answers previously displayed. The question is displayed on the board, and if a student has that answer on his board then he covers that square with a marker. Play continues until a student gets five in a row, either diagonally, vertically, or horizontally.

Trashketball

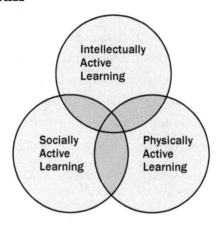

Trashketball is an easy game to incorporate and a tried-and-true favorite. The teacher asks students a question and gives everyone time to discuss the answer with their team members. Once students have a sufficient amount of time, the teacher randomly calls on a student to answer on behalf of his or her team. If the student gets the answer correct, a representative of the team gets to come to the front and shoot the "trashball" at the trash can. The team gets a point if the student makes the basket. The teacher can mark a two-point line and a three-point line and allows the students to select from which line they want to shoot.

Wheel of Fortune

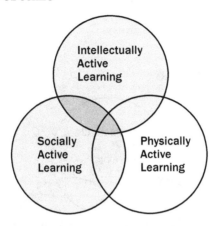

This is an easy game that requires basically no planning and can turn a worksheet into a game in seconds. The teacher creates a puzzle on the board by drawing blanks. For example:

___ ___ ___ ___ ___ ___ ___

___ ___ ___ ___ ___ ___   ___ ___ ___ ___ ___,

___ ___ ___ ___ ___ ___ ___ ___ ___ ___,

___ ___ ___   ___ ___ ___ ___ ___

___ ___ ___ ___ ___ ___ ___.

After students discuss the answer to a question or problem on a worksheet, the teacher randomly calls on a team. If the team answers the question correctly, they get to guess a letter in the puzzle. Students need not buy a vowel as in the real Wheel of Fortune rules because that is just too much hassle and hard to keep up with, so allow them to select any letter they wish. Once a team has selected a letter they can attempt to solve the puzzle if they wish. Of course, the team that solves the puzzle wins. In case you are wondering, the solution to the above example is, "Adverbs modify verbs, adjectives, and other adverbs." The puzzle solution should be a key concept.

Fly Swatter Game

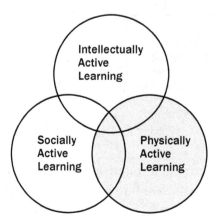

This is a favorite game that teachers have been using for years. After the teacher divides the class into teams, one player from each team comes up to the front of the room and, with their backs turned to the board holds a fly swatter while facing the class. The teacher has randomly written words or phrases on the board. The teacher asks a question and when she gives the signal, the students turn and the first person to swat the correct answer with his or her fly swatter earns a point for the team.

Quiz Bowl

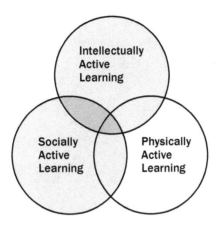

Quiz Bowl has been around for many years. Two teams of 4–5 students are at the front of the room at any given time. All the teams in the class rotate through the position of being at the front several times. When a team is seated at the front, each player has a buzzer. Buzzer systems made just for this purpose can be purchased online. Lacking the funds for that, teachers can purchase different noisemakers at a dollar store. One student might have a squeaky toy, one student might have a tambourine, one student might have a whistle, etc. Teachers must be able to distinguish by the sound which student "buzzed in" first. The teacher asks a question. When students think they know the answer, they sound their buzzers. If the student that buzzed in first answers correctly, then his or her team gets a more challenging question to discuss. The team earns a point for answering the challenge question correctly. If they are incorrect, the other team gets an opportunity to steal. Then two new teams rotate to the front seats.

Electronic Game Templates

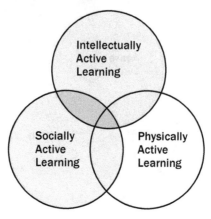

There are numerous free electronic game templates that can be found online and downloaded. Teachers simply enter their own questions and answers to suit their students' needs. These games are patterned after well-known games that many people are familiar with such as: Jeopardy, Who Wants to Be a Millionaire, Connect Four, and Are You Smarter Than a Fifth Grader?

Practical Suggestions

Ensuring Continuous On-Task Behavior from the Whole Class

Always make it possible for the other teams to steal the points if the team whose turn it is answers their question incorrectly. This gives all of the students in the class the motivation to pay attention and try to answer every question and also encourages learning from others' mistakes. An efficient way to do this is to give each team a dry-erase board to write the answer. When the first team misses the question, the teacher asks the other teams to hold up their answers simultaneously

on cue. Every team that has the correct answer gets
the points.

Keeping Score

Designate a student to be the scorekeeper and have them
keep the score on the board for everyone to see. This
eliminates you having to cognitively keep one more thing
going on in your head while you are trying to referee a
game...not an easy task. It also prevents arguing over the
score later, because everyone sees the scores while they are
being calculated. This prevents Johnny from complaining,
"We got the answer correct for #7 but we didn't get the points
15 minutes ago!"

Giving Prizes

Frankly, games are just more fun if there is an actual prize at
the end. The joy of winning brings satisfaction, but a prize
just makes it even better. Consider using a token system in
which students can turn in their tokens for rewards such as
sitting where they want at lunch, homework passes, special
seating in the classroom, etc.

Calling on Students

Depending on how you have structured the game, you may
call on students randomly, rather than going in order of
teams. This keeps it a little unpredictable and students feel
they must work on every question because they never know
when their name or their team will be called to provide an
answer. The old-fashioned name generator that teachers
have used for years is popsicle sticks. Every student's name is
written on a popsicle stick and placed in a cup. The teacher
has a different cup for each class and just randomly draws

a stick out. Return each stick after drawing it so that the student needs to continue paying attention. In addition, there are electronic random name generators such as Classtools. net, which has a name generator. Several apps are available for tablets such as List Selector, which allows teachers to randomly select students one-at-a-time, but will also randomly put students into groups of whatever size the teacher selects. Additionally, Pick Me! is a good app because the teacher can keep a record of whether an individual student got a question correct or not. It will give a report of how many questions a student got correct out of how many questions the student was asked, which is good formative assessment data.

Conclusion

Games are not the sole answer to student apathy—you need not play a game in every class. Not the only method of getting students engaged in active learning, they are simply one tool in a pedagogical toolbox. Games can be motivating for students and can get students taking on more of an intellectual challenge than they might be willing to do otherwise. Consider incorporating some games here and there into your instruction. But an important factor is that any game must be purposeful and must be useful in helping your students master your content objectives.

By the way, while this should not be our motivation, games are also fun for the teacher. Having some time set aside during a class period in which you can play while learning and laugh together with your students breaks up the monotony and helps deepen the relationship between teachers and students.

Chapter 7
Using Technology

No, you never get any fun out of the things you haven't done.
~Ogden Nash

This chapter focuses on using technology for the purpose of active learning. An example of such a strategy is students' creating a multimedia presentation to demonstrate their learning rather than using technology to efficiently process factual information. Depending on the technology students use and their purpose for using it, any given activity could involve one or more of the three dimensions (intellectual, social, or physical).

A given technology could fall anywhere on the active learning framework, but most often hits the intellectual and social dimensions. Technology used to gather data may also require students to get up and move around and, therefore, also enters the physically active learning dimension. But most classroom technology applications involve students sitting at a tablet or computer, so most technology applications fall in the intellectually active dimension, the socially active dimension, or both.

Intellectually Active

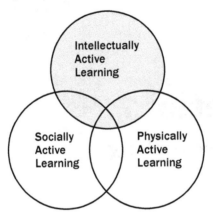

Teachers can incorporate intellectually active learning into technology activities by increasing the challenge of the lesson. If students apply what they are learning to new circumstances or to create new products, they are intellectually active in their learning:

Socially Active

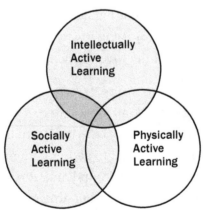

Activities in which students collaborate in small teams or with partners to create digital products intersect with the socially active circle.

Value of Using Technology in the Middle Grades Classroom

The World Has Changed

Technology has changed not only the way we interact with each other, but also our ability to create and the way we learn. We can access information anywhere with multiple devices and can interact with people across the globe on any topic we wish through online collaboration and online groups and chats.

Our economy has changed as well. The U.S. economy first centered on agriculture, then manufacturing became more critical, then service. Now, the economy is becoming increasingly dependent on innovation. Our current students must become future leaders who are able to generate new ideas and create new technologies that other countries need and want (Wagner, 2012).

Better Way to Learn

The ability to use technology to design, to create, and to communicate coincides perfectly with the young adolescent's natural inclination for active learning by doing. One of the best reasons for incorporating active learning through technology is the ability to go deeper in the content, to work with the content, and to create by using technological tools. Simply put, students find technology engaging, so teachers can use that to their advantage to get them engaged in content. Middle grades students need to be able to use technology to gather information, to communicate, to show what they have learned, to extend their social experiences, and to create (Partnership for 21st Century Skills, 2006). Our young adolescents need a level of digital literacy in order to function effectively in this world. Instead of memorizing endless facts, they need the ability to retrieve information, to verify its authenticity and credibility, to analyze that information, to think critically about that information, and apply it to new situations.

Good Fit for Young Adolescents

It is no surprise to middle grades experts that young adolescents are drawn to social networking sites, which fits perfectly with their social development. Because they are peer-oriented, interacting with peers in an online world that is not always viewable to their parents or teachers is a middle school student's dream-come-true. Online communication also expands their network of peers beyond those in their local neighborhood and school.

Early adolescence is actually a great time for students to use technology to learn. Becoming increasingly more comfortable with technology, middle graders are becoming more independent and have the cognitive ability to connect with technology in meaningful ways to learn (Bishop & Downes, 2013). The ability to access any information they wish is desirable to them, because knowledge fosters independence, which young adolescents desire.

Actually, middle grades students often have to downshift when they go into the classroom. Prensky (2001) coined the term "digital native" to describe the world in which our students have grown up. Downes & Bishop (2012) describe the world of a digital native this way:

> When faced with questions, students today find answers within seconds using Google or other search engines. When they want to acquire a new skill, they watch a YouTube video to learn it. When requiring further consultation, they tap into an electronic forum or social network that provides them access to myriad others who share their interests. (p.7)

While their world outside of school is primarily digital, school often feels "old-fashioned." The other day I sat in a café at a table beside a mom and four young adolescent girls. While all four girls spent the whole lunchtime on their smartphones, the mom just stared off in space. Asking those four girls to complete a worksheet in science class tomorrow does not honor the world that engages them. Young adolescents have grown accustomed to relevant content presented in an engaging and interactive way through high quality graphics with music in the background and videos. Having the ability to multi-task and switch quickly from application to application, worksheets just don't cut it for them. In a survey of 400 sixth, seventh, and eighth, grade students, students preferred activities that involved using computers and researching on the Internet. The activities they liked least were listening to teachers explain things and doing worksheets (Spires, Lee, Turner, & Johnson, 2008). We need to close the gap between students' out-of-school technological world and their in-school world.

Prepare Them for the Workplace

We need to prepare our middle grades students for the world they will face tomorrow, not the world we grew up in yesterday. Baker, Pearson, & Rozendal (2010) contend, "If our schools continue to limit the literacy curriculum to reading and writing traditional, alphabetic, printed texts, then our children will be well prepared for 1950 but ill-prepared for 2050" (p. 2). Because many of the jobs our students will hold have not even been created yet, this is a daunting task—we cannot imagine the technology they will use as adults in 20 years. We can, however, teach them to think critically, to be problem solvers, to be creative, and to be innovative. Wagner (2012) proposes seven survival skills that your students will need to be employable:

1. Critical thinking and problem solving
2. Collaboration across networks and leading by influence
3. Agility and adaptability
4. Initiative and entrepreneurship
5. Accessing and analyzing information
6. Effective oral and written communication
7. Curiosity and imagination

Using a textbook chapter to find answers for a worksheet probably is not going to help students attain these survival skills. Active learning through technology will.

Types of Technology

Students can now, with relative ease, create things that required advanced programming skills in the past. When planning activities, teachers must distinguish between Type I and Type II technologies. Type I technologies basically do more efficiently what teachers used to do by hand. For example, using a PowerPoint instead of a transparency on an overhead projector, using a grading program rather than the green gradebook and a pencil, or reading something online rather than reading a textbook. Although there is no downside to using technology to improve efficiency, quality, and accuracy, the real power of technology is in Type II technologies. Type II technologies enable students to do activities and tasks that they could not perform without technology. Type II technologies are about active acquisition of knowledge and creation of new ideas through application and innovation. Examples of Type II technologies are simulations, digital storytelling, and video production (Maddux, Johnson, & Willis, 2001).

The evolution of Internet use shows how technology use has shifted. The first version of the Internet, Web 1.0, was characterized by one-way delivery of information. The general public could access a wide-range of information by viewing what others had posted. The present, Web 2.0 version, allows users to interact with that information by creating websites, pages, and blogs to share with the world at large. Not long ago, users had to purchase software to do anything on the computer. Now, by simply logging onto the Internet, users apply Web 2.0 tools to create videos, stories, posters, and web pages. An amazing number of applications allow users to create things for free and an even greater number of sites allow users to do things for a small price, much cheaper than the rudimentary software schools formerly purchased. Web 2.0 applications allow teachers to take advantage of whatever hardware is available to them and their students, whether it is a computer lab, a class set of laptops, tablets, or bring-your-own device. In schools where every student does not have a device, teachers can place them in groups or use one or two classroom computers as a learning station. Because of the convenience and relatively low expense of Web 2.0 applications, technology is now more available than ever in the typical middle grades classroom.

Students need freedom and direction to use and express their knowledge in new and exciting ways. Teachers must utilize the technology tools available to not only capture the attention of our students but also to move them beyond memorization drills of endless facts. We need to get our students authentically engaged in real world problem solving and application and innovation. Allow them to actively learn, to digitally express themselves, and to create.

What Students Can Do

With the technology available in middle schools today, classrooms once again have the potential to be places of creativity and innovation. The middle grades classroom can become a place where students collaborate together to learn in ways that were unimaginable a decade or two ago. Technology allows students to explore ideas in a variety of ways to show what they have learned in creative ways (Martinez & Stager, 2013). The International Society for Technology in Education (ISTE) has four standards that describe what students need to be able to do with technology in order to be productive in a global and digital society:

1. *Creativity and innovation*—students need to be able to generate new ideas and create new products. They need to be able to study patterns and trends to make predictions and to explore complex issues.

2. *Communication and collaboration*—students need to be able to collaborate with others digitally to solve

problems and to communicate with a wide range of audiences using a variety of media.

3. *Research and information fluency*—students need to be able to gather, evaluate, and use information and to be able to process data and accurately report results.

4. *Critical thinking, problem solving, and decision making*—students need to be able to use a variety of digital tools to gather information, analyze data, and consider multiple perspectives to solve authentic problems (ISTE, 2015).

The Common Core Standards also emphasize digital literacy and being able to communicate via technology. The writing standards embed technology by expecting students to use a variety of digital tools, produce electronic text as well as multimedia presentations, collaborate and communicate with others, and use multimedia to scaffold their understanding of texts (Karchmer-Klein, 2013).

Obstacles vs Opportunities

Teachers are often quick to point out the challenges with incorporating technology into the classroom; however, when the veil is pulled back, the challenges have been minimized greatly in recent years. One common complaint is that not all students have computers or Internet access at home, when in fact, research shows that students use the Internet more at home than they do at school. In 2010, over half a decade ago, 93% of middle grades students had a computer at home and 84% had access to the Internet. Most troubling is that only 20% of those students went online at school. Simply, students were using technology out of school but were not being allowed to use technology in school to learn, even when that technology was available in their school (Rideout, Foehr, & Roberts, 2010). Take a poll of your students, you may be surprised. Ask them how many have access to the Internet through their phones, at their homes, or through their neighbors, their grandmothers, or the local library. If students have ample time including weekends to make arrangements to use the Internet, they may be able to work on at-home projects, with just a few needing school time for research. But even if having students use technology at home is difficult, teachers can have them work in groups on one device. Writing grants to obtain more technology for classrooms is another option.

The opportunities that technology brings certainly override the obstacles to getting it. Research has demonstrated that middle grades students are more motivated and more engaged in learning when using technology. Downes and Bishop (2012) found that the middle grades students in their project described many benefits to using technology to learn including higher engagement, organization and management of tasks, and efficiency. The key factor was the teacher's willingness to take risks. One of the teachers was quoted as saying, "The shift isn't in the students. The shift is in the teachers. We don't have to convince the students that this is the way to learn" (p. 14).

The most influential person determining whether technology will be used for active learning vs. passive drilling of facts is the teacher. Ensure that your students are using Type II technologies to actively construct their learning. This chapter provides some examples of free or inexpensive Web 2.0 tools to get your students actively learning using technology. There are seemingly unlimited tools out there; many are free and new ones are created almost daily. Any of these technologies can be used to teach different content in various subject areas. Be flexible with the technologies and adapt them to suit your purposes and your style.

Digital Storytelling

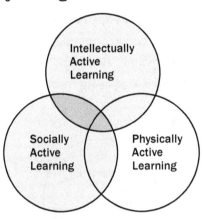

Digital storytelling requires students to compose a product using a variety of media including pictures, text, video, audio, and music. Using the media requires students to conceptualize the content in a way that allows them to present the key ideas using technology. The story could be students' own ideas and writing or it could be an explanation of a concept they have learned about. Digital storytelling involves a variety of media literacies including expository writing, speaking, digital production, and art. It cultivates imagination and creativity in your students as well as engagement (Bishop & Downes, 2013; Karchmer-Klein, 2013; Ohler, 2008)

A variety of applications allow students to create digital stories with relative ease. Voki.com allows them to create a talking animated avatar. Goanimate.com, moovly.com, and educreations (iPad app) allow students to create an animated video. Animoto.com allows them to turn still pictures into a video that incorporates text and music. Sock puppets (iPad app) allows students to create an animated puppet show with your students being the voices of the puppets. The puppets can explain anything you need to know about any topic you are studying. Show Me (iPad app) allows them to create a digital lesson and Storybird.com enables your students to create a digital storybook. Basically, any topic could be explained digitally in an engaging manner using these tools.

Digital Posters

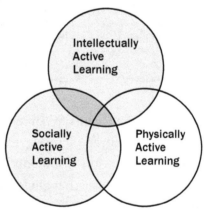

Forget the poster board and markers and allow students to demonstrate what they have learned about a topic using 21st century skills. Much more engaging for the digital natives in the middle grades, an example of an application that makes developing digital posters easy is edu.glogster.com, which gives students the ability to create a multimedia interactive electronic poster. Also, easel.ly is a theme-based web app for creating infographics and data visualizations.

Prezis

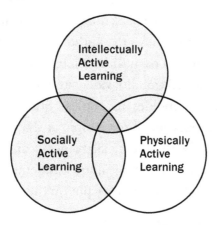

Students can use Prezi.com, a PowerPoint alternative, to create a visual aid for a presentation about a topic. It has all of the capabilities of PowerPoint, yet it is not quite so linear. Students can import images, videos, audio, and weblinks, but can do it more creatively than with PowerPoint. Rather than just moving from one slide to another, students can move across a blank canvas. The technology also features zooming in and out as well as rotating objects. Try asking your students to create a Prezi about a particular topic, and you will be amazed at what they produce.

Voicethread

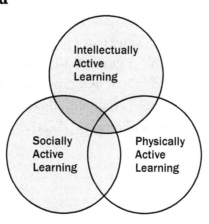

Voicethread.com allows students to create a digital presentation that incorporates images, videos, audio, and text. The application allows the author to make audio, video, and text comments on each slide, but it also has settings where others can make audio, video, and text comments on each slide. The possibilities are endless. Students can create a multimedia presentation about a topic or share their writing. They can interact with others electronically and get feedback on their ideas. This technology allows students to have a conversation about whatever they put on their slide.

Digital Graphic Organizers

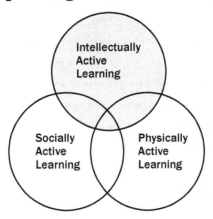

Sites such as bubbl.us and inspiration.com allow students to create graphic organizers and concept maps digitally. Students can use graphic organizers to make sense of ideas gathering in their heads about new topics they are learning. Creating graphic organizers digitally allows students to easily share them with others and revisit and revise them as new learning occurs.

Digital Cartoon Strips

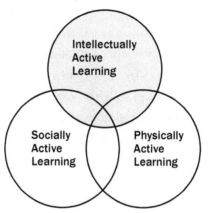

Who doesn't like a good old-fashioned cartoon strip? That just brings great fun into learning any topic. Several applications such as pixton.com and readwritethink.org make it easy for your students to create cartoon characters with dialog about the concept they are studying.

Cube Creator

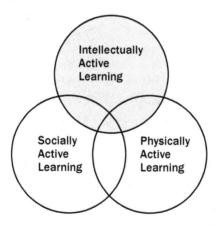

Readwritethink.org has many different interactive tools, but one that is particularly well-suited for different content areas in the middle grades is Cube Creator. The website has four different templates, a bio cube, a mystery cube, a story cube, and a create-your-own cube. The cubes have prompts on each side that students respond to with both text and images. This is a good tool for both summarizing and synthesizing, but it also allows for creativity as students or their teachers can modify the prompts on the sides of the cubes.

Fakebook

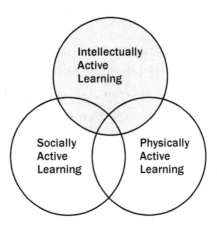

Fakebook is a play on Facebook without the inherent dangers of the actual social network. Fakebook, which is a free application found on classtools.net, allows a student to create a fake Facebook page for a character. This could be a character in a novel, a scientist, a historical figure, or anyone fictional or otherwise. The student also creates friends for the Fakebook profile so other experts or people of the time period or other characters in the novel can make comments on the main person's page. Students can demonstrate what they know about the topic through the conversation they create on the page.

Blogs

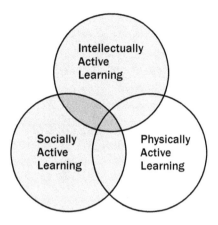

Weblogs, which are more commonly known as blogs, allow students to create and share electronic journals that incorporate text, images, video, and audio. Since blogs are shared via the Internet, readers can comment on entries and allow conversations between the author and the audience. Teachers can specifically prompt students for responses or allow more freedom in their choice of topics. Many Web 2.0 tools such as Edublogs provide virtual spaces for this purpose (Karchmer-Klein, 2013).

Conclusion

Bringing technology into the middle grades classroom just makes sense from an active learning perspective. First, it connects with the natural inclinations of the digital natives seated in the classroom. Since they are comfortable with technology and use it for every other purpose in life, why not allow them to use it for learning? Second, technology is an engaging way to get young adolescents involved in active learning. By focusing on Type II technologies, students create products of high quality while they are learning.

Part Three

Introduction

What Active Learning Looks Like in the Classroom

Hopefully, you are sold by this point on the importance of getting your students engaged in active learning. But it helps to have a picture of what this really looks like and how it really works. Part 3 makes the connection between active learning instructional strategies and the content of middle grades language arts, mathematics, science, and social studies.

Part 3 also gives teachers examples of how four different teachers incorporate active learning in real classrooms. These are real teachers in real classrooms with real kids...hormones and all. They are from different school systems and from very different settings: urban, rural, and suburban. They all have their own styles and personalities. Some use humor and some are all business. They all make active learning happen in different ways. Hopefully, you can picture this happening in your classroom as well.

Chapter 8

Active Learning in the Middle Grades Mathematics Classroom

Some teachers could do more for their students by not doing so much for them. ~Anonymous

When you picture the traditional middle school mathematics class in your mind, it probably goes something like this:

1. The teacher goes over the answers to the homework

2. The teacher demonstrates a few problems of the new skill on the board.

3. The students practice about 20 similar problems at their seats while the teacher walks around and assists students as needed.

4. If time is left, students begin the homework assignment, which is similar to the classwork assignment they just completed.

Sound familiar?

Today's middle grades classroom should look very different. No, we are not suggesting the teacher should never demonstrate a problem, the students should never practice a math skill, and homework should be abolished. However, it is necessary to take the focus off of the teacher and move it to the students. Students should engage in active learning during math class, and they should be intellectually, socially, and physically active.

Intellectually Active: What the Mathematics Experts Say

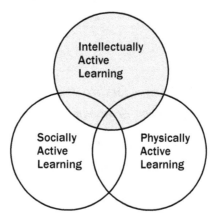

Active learning is fundamental to meeting the needs of young adolescents, and the National Council of Teachers of Mathematics (NCTM) has long advocated for methodologies that require students to be intellectually engaged in constructing new knowledge with conceptual understanding (2000). Active learning instructional strategies such as problem-solving tasks, questioning, and inquiry are ideal for this.

An important theme in the literature related to mathematical problem solving is the cognitive demand that a task requires of students. Stein, Smith, Henningsen, and Silver (2009) offer a framework for looking at the cognitive demands of tasks. Low cognitive demand tasks require that students demonstrate memorized knowledge or perform procedures without connections to any context. High cognitive demand tasks require higher levels of cognitive demand and mathematical reasoning. Students need to attach meaning to the mathematics and make connections among different representations. In order for students to be intellectually active in their learning, it is important for teachers to select problem-solving tasks that require higher levels of cognitive demand.

Mathematical Practices

Middle grades mathematics teachers can use several strategies to keep the cognitive demand high and to ensure that their students remain intellectually active. Teachers should expect students to regularly use the mathematical practices as recommended in the Common Core State Standards for Mathematics (National Governors Association Center for Best Practices and Council of Chief State School Officers, 2015). When students follow these mathematical practices, they are intellectually active in their learning of mathematics:

> *Make sense of problems and persevere in solving them—* Instead of randomly trying out operations or solutions, students first try to understand the problem and begin approaching the problem from a logical entry point. If they do not immediately uncover the correct solution, they do not give up. Using mathematical logic, they continue to approach the problem based on what they already know. Because they are not just employing

the solution path that was just presented to them by the teacher, this process requires students to be intellectually active.

Reason abstractly and quantitatively—When students represent a given problem in a symbolic manner, they are intellectually active. Students manipulate an abstract representation and then apply its symbols to a specific problem at hand while considering whether their computations make sense in terms of the given context.

Construct viable arguments and critique the reasoning of others—Intellectually active students make conjectures and then test those conjectures using a variety of means such as prior mathematical knowledge, counterexamples, and inductive reasoning. They are able to make generalizations and justify their conclusions using mathematical reasoning. But intellectually active middle grades students are also able to consider how their classmates are reasoning about a concept and to ask questions or suggest mathematical arguments if they think their classmates have a flaw in their reasoning.

Model with mathematics—Intellectually active students are flexible in how they model a mathematics problem. They are able to use a variety of approaches such as simplifying a complex situation and then using mathematical reasoning to extrapolate to the given problem. They are able to analyze relationships and draw conclusions. They are comfortable using diagrams, graphs, tables, and formulas to model a given problem.

Use appropriate tools strategically—Middle grades mathematics students use a variety of tools including, technology, manipulatives, measurement devices, and good old-fashioned paper. Using these tools in meaningful ways such as challenging assumptions, making predictions, posing new problems, and exploring mathematical concepts in a deeper way requires students to be intellectually active.

Attend to precision—Intellectual activity involves accurate use of terminology, units of measure, and symbols. Middle grades mathematics students precisely communicate their mathematical reasoning.

Look for and make use of structure—Intellectually active students look for patterns in numbers and computations they work with so they can make generalizations or mathematical arguments based on those patterns. Middle grades students apply organization and structure in problem-solving situations and do not just randomly and haphazardly start substituting numbers or trying computations.

Look for and express regularity in repeated reasoning—If middle grades mathematics students are intellectually active, they will begin to notice repeated calculations and find general methods or shortcuts to save time and effort. They evaluate the reasonableness of their results and then react accordingly.

Mathematics Teaching Practices

How do teachers get students to consistently employ the mathematical practices? What should middle grades mathematics teachers do so they can get their students intellectually active and engaged? NCTM recommends eight mathematics teaching practices:

Establish mathematics goals to focus learning—"Effective teaching of mathematics establishes clear goals for the mathematics that students are learning, situates goals within learning progressions, and uses the goals to guide instructional decisions" (NCTM, 2014, p.10).

The teacher must know what the long-term math goal is and what concept students must understand by the end of the period. If the teacher does not know where he or she is leading the class, both teacher and students will wander around aimlessly and unproductively and never get anywhere.

- After determining the goal, the teacher plans and selects activities that will build on each other to scaffold students' understanding of the concept.

- Everything on the lesson plan should be clearly on a path that leads to the goal. Asking students to engage in fun activities that are merely fluff and are not in line with the selected goal will lead students astray.

Implement tasks that promote reasoning and problem solving— "Effective teaching of mathematics engages students in solving and discussing tasks that promote mathematical reasoning and problem solving and allow multiple entry points and varied solution strategies" (NCTM, 2014, p.10).

- Not all tasks are created equal. Be a task connoisseur. Collect good tasks related to your standards wherever you can...professional development, curriculum modules, textbooks, the Internet, other teachers, or any other resource you can find.

- The priority is to find high quality tasks. If an activity has one obvious solution pathway, pass it by. Find tasks that can be approached using a variety of strategies.

Use and connect mathematical representations—"Effective teaching of mathematics engages students in making connections among mathematical representations to deepen understanding of mathematics concepts and procedures and as tools for problem solving" (NCTM, 2014, p.10).

- It is important, at least once each day, to have a math problem with the concrete representation (manipulatives), the visual representation (diagram, graph, table, etc.) and the abstract/symbolic representation (the equation) on the board simultaneously. It is critical to lead students to see the particular aspects of the problem in the various representations. For example, "We have the expression $5x + 6$. Where can I see the 5 in the cubes? Where can I see the 5 in the table?"

- It is also important to make connections between mathematical concepts. For example, students are often amazed that square numbers actually make squares. Therefore, it is possible to discuss area of rectangles at the same time you are discussing exponents. Making those connections (or asking students to make those connections) can deepen conceptual understanding.

Facilitate meaningful mathematical discourse—"Effective teaching of mathematics facilitates discourse among students to build shared understanding of mathematical ideas by analyzing and comparing student approaches and arguments" (NCTM, 2014, p.10).

- The best strategy to accomplish meaningful discourse with your students is to be genuinely interested in how they are thinking about the problem. Really listen to your students and you will be fascinated by what is going on in their brains. You will also find strategies and solution paths that you had never considered, but that actually work.

- When students are working on a problem, whether in groups or individually, walk around and notice the different approaches they are using. Make a note of 3-4 students that you will ask to put their solutions on the board. Have them present their solutions in order from the least advanced to the most mathematically advanced and elegant solution. Then ask the class to make connections between the different approaches.

Pose purposeful questions—"Effective teaching of mathematics uses purposeful questions to assess and advance students' reasoning and sense making about important mathematical ideas and relationships" (NCTM, 2014, p.10).

- Write questions into your lesson plans. High level, purposeful questions do not just appear in your mind while you are trying to juggle 30 middle grades students and multiple tasks. Think of and write down good questions ahead of time that will challenge student thinking.

- Try to predict the errors students might make or incorrect pathways students might take. Think of questions or counterexamples you can ask that will prevent them from getting stymied or becoming convinced that the wrong path they are on will lead them to the pot of gold.

Build procedural fluency from conceptual understanding— "Effective teaching of mathematics builds fluency with procedures on a foundation of conceptual understanding so that students, over time, become skillful in using procedures flexibly as they solve contextual and mathematical problems" (NCTM, 2014, p.10).

- The important thing here is the order. Start with an activity that has students really exploring the mathematical concept in depth. Work on conceptual understanding first and then develop procedural fluency.

- Once the students have some ideas about the solution and how they got there, it is important for the teacher to make sure the class understands the key ideas related to the concept. At this point students do the traditional taking notes in a math notebook but the notes are agreed upon together as a class, not just given by the teacher.

- The last step is to build the procedural fluency. After the students have a conceptual understanding of the math, then they practice and improve their efficiency at applying the procedure. But the procedure now makes sense to students rather than becoming a bunch of confusing steps they have to memorize.

- We are teachers because we like to help people. Helping is good and a generous thing to do. But consider what help actually is. If the teacher jumps in and rescues students too quickly, they will watch the teacher solve the problem and remain helpless. If students figure out how to solve it and own it themselves, they have learned how to be an independent thinker and problem solver.

Elicit and use evidence of student thinking—"Effective teaching of mathematics uses evidence of student thinking to assess progress toward mathematical understanding and to adjust instruction continually in ways that support and extend learning" (NCTM, 2014, p.10).

- Teachers cannot make judgments about whether students are understanding concepts based on the number of their correct answers. Asking students questions, either verbally or in writing, and getting them to tell you how they found the answer becomes the starting point to fine tune instruction by focusing on the specific misunderstandings. This is much more efficient than just repeating the same information.

Theory into Action—Examples of Intellectually Active Instructional Strategies for Middle Grades Mathematics Topics

The following chart offers examples of instructional strategies to get students intellectually active as they explore mathematics. There are examples across a range of middle grades mathematics topics but many of these strategies can easily be adapted to fit other mathematics topics as well.

Topic	Activity
Absolute Value	*Journal Question*—Why is the absolute value of a number always positive? Provide a written explanation of your reasoning along with a diagram to support your thinking.
Scientific Notation	*The Scientist Shortcut*—In this inquiry activity students discover the rules for translating numbers between scientific notation and standard form.

The Scientist Shortcut Task
Because scientists have to work with really long numbers all the time, they use a shorthand way of writing them. See if you can find the trick.

Numbers Bigger Than One

Long Way	Shortcut
93,000,000	9.3 x 107
147,000	1.47 x 105
1,088,700,000	1.0887 x 109
5,000	5 x 103
10,300,000,000,000	1.03 x 1013

Numbers Between Zero and One

Long Way	Shortcut
.000076	7.6 x 10-5
.0104	1.04 x 10-2
.000000006	6 x 10-9
.00000052	5.2 x 10-7
.00000000010300	1.03 x 10-10

What do you think is the rule for writing the short versions of the numbers?

Circumference of a Circle	*Circle Scavenger Hunt*—Students measure diameters of various circular objects with string. The students count how many strings it takes to equal the circumference of each circle. Students should notice that the circumference is always a little more than three times the diameter. Through whole class discussion, the teacher ensures that the class derives the formula that the circumference of a circle is ∏ x d.
Real Numbers	*Number Scavenger Hunt*—Find and cut out different numbers from newspapers or online articles. Here is the list of numbers the students must find: 1. A natural number between 100 and 200. 2. A whole number less than 10. 3. A whole number greater than one million. 4. An integer less than 0. 5. A rational number that is expressed as a terminating decimal. 6. A rational number that is expressed as a fraction. 7. A rational number that is expressed as an integer. 8. An irrational number that is expressed as a decimal. 9. An irrational number that is expressed as a square root. 10. A real number between 0 and 1. 11. A number expressed as a percent that is greater than 100. 12. A fraction that would convert to a decimal between 0 and .75. 13. A decimal that would convert to a fraction between ½ and ¾. 14. An integer less than -100. 15. A rational number between 10 and 11.

Algebraic Equations	*Word Problems Story Book*—Students create a book of word problems that match given algebraic equations. Note: the teacher can easily use this activity for differentiation by requiring specific students to select a specific set of equations. Also students can use storybird.com to make electronic books.

Story Word Problems Book
Choose one of the sets of four equations below. Write four story problems, with the same theme, to exactly match the four equations (one story for each equation).

Set A
$x + 5 = 23$
$3x = 21$
$2x + 3 = 11$
$3x - 6 = 18$

Set B
$x + 2.5 = 81$
$x = 6$
$3x - 2 = 29$
$x + 13 = 15$

1. Create a cover for your book. Create a title for your book and establish a theme. Illustrate the cover to match the theme.

2. Present your project in book form. Create one page per problem, including the problem, the solution to the problem showing each step, and the check of the problem. Illustrate each story problem. Be sure to use complete sentences and correct grammar, spelling, and punctuation. Be sure that each story really does translate into the given equation. |

Properties of Quadrilaterals	*Venn Diagram*—Students create a Venn diagram showing the relationships among quadrilaterals (e.g., all squares are rectangles, but not all rectangles are squares.) The finished product should look something like this:
Slope	*Chain Note*—The teacher arranges the students into groups of four. Each student in each group of four receives a different one of four chain notes with each chain note representing a different line. They are given two coordinates on the line. The first person draws the graph, the second person makes a table, the third person writes the equation, and the fourth person records the slope of the line (Edwards, 2014).

Socially Active-What the Mathematics Experts Say

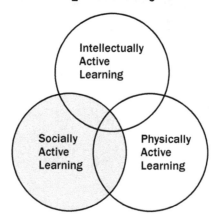

Mathematical discourse is a critical part of learning for middle grades mathematics students (Piccolo, Harbaugh, Carter, Capraro, & Capraro, 2008) and is the method of engaging students in socially active learning. Students interact with each other and with the teacher in a variety of ways to understand the mathematics. Students make conjectures, give explanations and mathematical arguments, and collaborate with their peers. Teachers should endeavor to build a sense of community in their classrooms where students feel safe to take risks and express their thinking. The community negotiates the mathematics and forms shared meanings (NCTM, 2000).

Interactions in the classroom foster community problem solving and reasoning. Problem solving empowers learners with strategies to approach new situations and gives them autonomy to try creative approaches. Such an approach de-emphasizes correctness of answers and the knowledge of the teacher. There is an environment of active knowing where students are engaged in contextual problems and teachers serve as facilitators and guides. In a mathematical community, students do this reasoning collaboratively. They struggle through concepts and defend their reasoning to their peers while learning from their classmates' ideas.

Through communicating their reasoning to each other, students are able to clarify mathematical ideas for themselves. The teacher's role in classroom discourse is to pose questions, listen carefully to the ideas of students, and encourage students to participate in productive mathematical discourse. The students' role in classroom discourse should be to communicate their reasoning, listen to the reasoning of others, and provide mathematical justification of their reasoning (NCTM, 1991).

Mathematical discourse is particularly important in a middle grades classroom. Since students are at a place in their emotional development where taking intellectual risks in a classroom setting may be difficult, teachers need to be sensitive to the needs of their students. It is important to create a classroom culture that is supportive and collaborative rather than critical and competitive. But be careful to establish the expectation that *all* of your students will talk about the mathematics, not just the outgoing students. Even if students are shy or reserved, teachers should expect them to communicate their mathematical knowledge (Bennett, 2014).

Theory into Action—Examples of Socially Active Instructional Strategies for Middle Grades Mathematics Topics

The following examples of instructional strategies get students socially active as they explore mathematics across a range of middle grades topics. However, there are no limits on the rich mathematics problems that students can solve through such methods.

Topic	Activity
Surface Area and Volume of Cylinders	*Soda Can Lab*—Students work in groups to determine the surface area and volume of a can of soda. (Note: Since the typical soda can has a beveled edge at the top, you will need to agree on whether you will go with the circumference of the can or the lid.) Once every student in the group can explain to the teacher how to find the surface area and volume, they are given a soda to drink while they complete the rest of the activity.

Soda Can Lab

1. Find the surface area of the soda can using centimeters. Be sure each member of the group can explain how you got this answer.

2. Find the volume of the soda can using centimeters. Be sure each member of the group can explain how you got this answer.

Once you have determined items 1 and 2 you will need to demonstrate your understanding to your teacher before receiving your soda and proceeding to items 3 and 4.

3. The company is thinking about changing the size of the can and wants to know if it would be cost-effective. What would happen to the volume of the can if the diameter doubled? Do you think this would be a good idea? Why or why not?

4. The company that produces this product would like to design a new label. What would the dimensions and area of this label have to be?

Area of Polygons and Proportional Reasoning	*Stained Glass Window Project*—Students work in groups to create designs for stained glass windows and determine how much glass will be needed for the finished product.

Stained Glass Window Project

You are working as a designer in a stained glass window company. The customer wants windows with patterns made up of only triangles, rectangles, and circles. Your task is to design a sample window using black construction paper (to represent the supports) and colored tissue paper (which will represent the glass). You may use as many of each shape as you want, but you must have at least one triangle, one rectangle, and one circle in your window. Design your window and then answer the following questions which will help the production department:

1. What is the area of one rectangle? How did you determine that?

2. What is the area of one triangle? How did you determine that?

3. What is the area of one circle? How did you determine that?

4. Determine what color each shape in your design will be and create a sample with construction paper and tissue paper.

5. List each color and how many square centimeters of that color are in the window.

6. The actual window size is five times larger than your sample. How much glass of each color will be needed for one window?

Making Predictions Based on Data from a Sample	*Concession Stand*—Have students work in groups to create a brief survey to determine what drinks to sell at the baseball concession stand and what price to sell them for. Have the students collect data from a random sample of students in the school. Students will also need to determine the likely attendance at the game. Given the cost of purchasing the drink per ounce, students must determine what type and how much of each drink to sell in the concession stand to make a profit.
Percents and Computation with Decimals	*Family Budget*—Assign small groups of students to families with one salary. Salaries are assigned randomly, so one family might have a lawyer's salary and another family might have a custodian's salary. Students are given a gross annual salary and have to compute percentages for taxes, social security, etc., working their way down to a net monthly income. Once they have the correct monthly income, students have to compute their utility bills, cable bills, etc. Then they are given options for housing, clothing, transportation, and so on, that they can select based on the amount left in their monthly budget.
Problem Solving	*Team Quiz Bowl*—Place a challenging word problem on the board and allow an appropriate number of minutes to find the solution. Every team works together to determine their answer, which they write on a student dry-erase board. The team whose turn it is shows their answer when time is up. If the answer is correct, the teacher randomly calls on someone from that team to justify the answer and, if done appropriately, the team gets a point. If that team misses the question, the other teams in the room are told to hold up their boards simultaneously. Every team with the correct answer gets a point.

Physically Active—What the Mathematics Experts Say

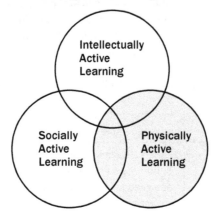

One method of physically active learning in the mathematics classroom is using manipulatives. While this involves limited physical movement, using manipulatives does allow students to have some hands-on, physical activity in the classroom, rather than just dealing with abstract representations of mathematical concepts. Researchers have found that using manipulatives to assist students in learning mathematics can have a positive effect if used with the appropriate instructional techniques. Manipulatives can aid students in retention, problem solving, transfer, and justification (Carbonneau, Marley, & Selig, 2013).

An exciting movement that gets students physically active during mathematics class is the move towards more science, technology, engineering, and mathematics (STEM) programs. STEM projects not only integrate concepts across disciplines, but they often require students to create a product. For example, Omundsen (2014) describes a STEM project on building boats out of cardboard that his middle grades students completed. The students were intellectually, socially, and physically active in the design and construction phases, which incorporated many skills across disciplines.

Examples of Physically Active Instructional Strategies

The following chart provides examples of instructional strategies to get students physically active as they explore mathematics. There are examples across a range of middle grades mathematics topics, and many of these strategies can be adapted to teach other mathematics topics as well.

Topic	Activity
Scatter Plots and Line of Best Fit	*Car Ramp Problem*—Students create ramps out of strips of thick cardboard and stacks of books, and they roll toy cars down the ramp, measuring how far the cars roll. The height of the ramp is adjusted by adding or taking away books and several trials are measured at each height. After collecting the data, the students graph the average length of the roll in relation to the height of the ramp and determine a line of best fit to make predictions about how far the car will roll at other heights.
Integers	*Integers Number Line*—The number line is an excellent representation for computation with integers. Consider creating a giant number line on the floor of your classroom using masking tape. Then allow students to actually walk through problems on the giant number line while students at their seats talk them through the problem.

Parallel Lines and Angle Relationships	*Streamers*—Use three crepe paper party streamers to represent two parallel lines and a transversal. Pairs of students hold the three streamers. Then have other pairs of students hold cards with two matching terms written on them and stand in the appropriate location. For example, two students might have cards that say "Alternate Exterior Angles". Each of the students would need to stand amidst the streamers in two angles that are on alternate sides of the transversal and are exterior to the parallel lines. Ask a different pair of students to take the same cards and stand in a different set of alternate exterior angles. Repeat this with other angle relationships. Once students have the vocabulary down, you can give one student a card with an angle measurement (e.g., 60°) and assign an angle for them to stand in. Other students are given cards that say either 60° or 120° and have to locate themselves in the appropriate angles. Students have to defend whether or not they are congruent to another given student and their reasoning based on the angle relationship.
Volume and Surface Area of Three-Dimensional Figures	*Build a Geometric Town*—Students construct buildings out of nets printed on construction paper in the shape of prisms, cylinders, pyramids, and cones. The buildings are connected together to make a city landscape. Students have to measure and find the surface area and volume of designated portions of the city such as a block on a given street.
Ordering Rational Numbers on a Number Line	*Cards with Numbers*—Each student is given a card with numbers in different forms: square roots, decimals, fractions, etc. They have to arrange themselves in order from least to greatest.

Coordinate Plane	*Classroom Coordinate Plane—*Arrange the student desks in rows. Put tape on the floor down the middle of the rows both vertically and horizontally to represent the axes of a coordinate plane. The desks would represent points. Have one student come to the front of the room and give them a card with an ordered pair written on it. The student has to go sit in that desk. The student who was originally sitting at that location goes to the front and is given a new ordered pair. This continues until all the students have had the opportunity to be a point on the coordinate plane.
Fractions/ Decimals/ Percents	*Four Corners—* Place a different decimal in each corner. Each student is given one of the four fractions or four percents that is equivalent to one of the four decimals, and they must find the correct corner.
Multiple Mathematics Topics	*Manipulatives—*Manipulatives allow for a small amount of physical movement and give students some hands-on opportunities. Examples appropriate for middle grades classrooms are: Fraction Towers Algebra Tiles Base Ten Blocks Cuisenaire Rods Cubes Integer Counters Geoboards Pattern Blocks Dice
Proportional Reasoning	*Wii—*Allow the students to play a Wii game such as Wii Sports Resort Canoeing, or another game on the Wii. Then ask proportional reasoning questions such as, "If you can canoe 65 yards in one minute, how far would you expect to be able to canoe in 20 minutes? Many other mathematics topics can be connected to Wii activities as well (Hearn & Winner, 2013).

Multiple Topics	*Task Cards*—Instead of passing out a worksheet with practice problems, consider cutting the sheet apart and pasting the problems on 4 x 6 cards. Put one problem on each card, and place the cards at stations around the room. Students may do the cards in different orders, but each student eventually rotates through all of the stations, until they have completed each problem.

What This Looks Like in a Real Middle Grades Mathematics Classroom

Katrina Norris (pseudonym), a participant in my research study, teaches in an inner-city school that is 96% African-American. Ninety-nine percent of the students in the school are on free- or reduced-lunch. Katrina runs a no-nonsense classroom and has very strong classroom management skills. Her students know that it is all business in her room. However, Katrina believes strongly in using a variety of learning approaches as she finds that different students respond to different things. She feels responsible for her students' learning and does not want any student to struggle with math as a result of the way she teaches it. One morning while they were working on subtracting mixed numbers, I observed Katrina's class, which was working on fractions that require regrouping. I have copied some excerpts from my observation notes below, and I have inserted (in italics) some of the thoughts I had while watching the lesson.

9:20 The class begins with their regular routine of a "Daily Number Talk". Katrina leads the class in a discussion of a problem on the board. She made these statements when her students had difficulty:

"It's okay if you aren't sure."
"What should Tyriq have done?"
"Let's try this one more time."
"This is an easy one."

Katrina constantly encouraged her students. I got the sense that these students had struggled in mathematics previously but were gaining confidence in Katrina's classroom. There was an atmosphere of patience and respect. The students were genuinely trying to get it.

[This first portion of the lesson would qualify as socially active learning because Katrina is leading a whole class discussion, and the students are working together to do the Number Talk.]

9:30 Katrina begins the next portion of the lesson by saying, "Yesterday we were talking about subtracting mixed numbers. We are going to go over it to jog your memory. It's not hard, you just have to get the hang of it." She has the students divide their page in their math journals into two sides *(this is obviously a regular routine and normal procedure the students are used to)*. The left side is the VIP section ("Very Important Problem") section. On that side of the page, the students copy the problem from the board:

$18\frac{1}{8} - 10\frac{1}{4}$

On the right side of the page, the students are to write the steps or explain what they are doing as they solve the problem. Katrina asks students questions as they work through the problem step-by-step together, constantly asking them to explain and justify their responses.

When they get to the core issue that Katrina wants to focus on today she says, "Now we have a problem. Can you take 2/8 from 1/8"? Several students say "no" and Katrina asks, "What do we do now"? This begins much debate that is finally resolved by Colby who convinces his classmates that regrouping is the way to go. The class finishes working through the problem together.

[This portion of the lesson would qualify as both social and intellectual activity. It is social activity, because the class is working through the problem together. It becomes intellectual activity at the point when Katrina requires the students to figure out themselves that they need to regroup, rather than just telling them that regrouping should be the next step.]

9:42 Katrina now displays the problem $7\,^1/_3 - 4\,^2/_3$. She sets a timer and all the students get busy working out the problem on their individual dry-erase boards. As the students are working, Katrina walks around and asks students individual questions. Students in other parts of the room help each other, which appears to be acceptable and part of the normal routine.

I can't help but notice the accountability. Every student is expected to do everything in the lesson and Katrina makes sure they do it. She does not let anyone off the hook.

When the timer goes off, Katrina calls on some students to talk her through the problem, spending quite a bit of time on the regrouping step.

9:59 In their regular groups, the students move to assigned stations. One group of students, assigned to a software program on the computer, practices subtracting mixed numbers.

Two groups of students at different places in the room play a board game, which also involves subtracting mixed numbers. And two groups of students at different sets of desks work out problems on dry-erase boards.

I believe she has differentiated the activities. I think the students playing the game are working with mixed numbers that already have a common denominator, but still need to regroup, while the problems given to the students with the dry-erase boards all seem to require both regrouping and finding a common denominator.

10:10 All the students in the class are doing math. Without any interference of learning, students have resolved a few disagreements at the game tables by giving players with incorrect answers the reasons their answers were wrong. Katrina is walking around the room and monitoring. It appears that the students are mostly getting their problems correct. Everyone has not reached mastery, but no one seems completely lost, either.

I perceive a calm energy in the air. The students seem to know that they will be busy working on math all period. No time has been wasted during this class period.

[The stations portion of the lesson is socially active learning for students working in the four groups (not for the students working at individual computers—but they do some physical activity as they move to their stations and play the games.]

10:15 Katrina tells everyone to clean up their areas and the bell rings shortly thereafter for the students to change classes.

You, like Katrina, can get your students engaged in active learning while they are digging into the mathematics concepts that you want them to learn. You can adapt the activities listed in this chapter along with previous chapters to get your students intellectually, socially, and physically active in your math classroom. If you are new to active learning instructional strategies, then just try one next week. Take small steps and you will soon be rewarded with engaged students who enjoy learning mathematics.

Chapter 9
Active Learning in the Middle Grades Language Arts Classroom

The more you do of what you've done, the more you'll have of what you've got. ~Anonymous

Educators think of the language arts as communication through reading, writing, speaking, listening, and viewing. Perhaps an image comes to your mind of a quiet library with everyone absorbed in a book, or maybe a coffee shop where you go to write in your journal, or a café with everyone communicating through laptops and tablets. I encourage you to think of getting your students actively engaged while they are improving their communication skills. It is vital for students to be intellectually active and thinking critically about what they read and hear. It is worthwhile for students to be socially active and to interact with each other and with the outside world as they are learning. It is also important for them to be physically active. Communication should be an active endeavor rather than a passive event.

Intellectually Active—What the Language Arts Experts Say

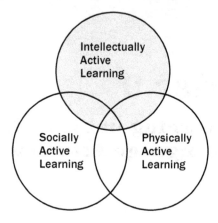

To promote young adolescents' intellectual development middle grades language arts teachers must set high expectations and empower students to think creatively. If teachers set high expectations, middle grades students will meet and often exceed those expectations. By allowing students to pursue engaging activities, they can learn how to research and find answers to questions that they pose, but also learn how to communicate their knowledge and ideas clearly to others.

In the middle grades, young adolescents should be making a shift from mastering basic literacy skills to more challenging processes of academic literacies. Those processes include interacting with a range of difficult texts, writing and communicating in different content areas, and engaging in disciplinary discourses using the academic language of different disciplines (National Council of Teachers of English, 2015). Students are moving beyond a literal comprehension of text and moving towards higher-order comprehension, which involves analysis, inference, evaluation, and reflective comprehension (Faber, 2006).

To assist middle grades students as they make this transition to higher literacy demands, the National Council of Teachers of English (NCTE) recommends a learner-centered approach that incorporates active, inquiry-based activities. Teachers should strive to connect literacy activities to authentic, real-world contexts, and students should have opportunities to ask their own questions and explore those questions using inquiry, critical thinking, and research skills. When possible, teachers should allow student decision making and encourage independent learning (NCTE, 2015).

One method of intellectual activity ideal for the middle grades language arts classroom is project-based learning using multimodal literacy. Jewitt and Kress (2003) define multimodal literacy as the ability to use different representational modes to make meaning, to communicate, to interact with, and to process information. Young adolescents are growing up with unprecedented access to different types of technology. It is possible in today's middle grades language arts classroom to allow students to learn and to create with a wide variety of digital media including images, sound, video, print, and music. Allowing students to create and represent what they are learning about a topic through digital storytelling or video production engages these digital natives in more powerful ways than traditional language arts textbooks might be able to do (Dreon, Kerper, & Landis, 2011; Spires, Hervey, Morris, & Stelpflug, 2012).

Theory into Action—Examples of Intellectually Active Instructional Strategies for Middle Grades Language Arts Topics

The following chart provides examples of instructional strategies to get students intellectually active as they explore literature and writing. The examples cross a range of middle grades language arts topics, and teachers can adapt many of these strategies to fit other language arts topics as well.

Topic	Activity
Writing Descriptive Sentences	*Write on Your Desk*—All students get a dry-erase marker and clear everything off their desks. The teacher displays an interesting and vivid picture on the board, and the students craft the best descriptive sentence they can about the picture. The students actually write on their desk with the marker. You will want to test this out first, but your student desks are probably dry-erase-marker-friendly. Students are more willing than usual to revise and edit because doing it with a dry-erase pen is more fun and easier than with pencil and paper. (This idea came from Tanya McLain, who teaches in Evans, Georgia.)
Informational Literacy	*Mind Map*—Put a picture that captures a concept in the middle of a paper. Create a concept map using bubbles and arrows of various topics related to the idea with details coming off of those topics. Students can do this digitally using bubbl.us or inspiration.com.

Writing with Precision	*Shades of Meaning*—Each student receives a paint chip from a hardware store with three to five different shades of a color. Students generate a continuum of terms associated with an idea. Allow the students to use a thesaurus and dictionary. For example, words associated with light include dim, glow, bright, dazzle, and glaring. The students write the words on the paint chip in order, with the strongest word on the deepest color (Fisher, Brozo, Frey, & Ivey, 2011). Example: Uneasy | Anxious | Frantic
Vocabulary	*Frayer Model Vocabulary Card*—Students receive a blank card and divide the card into four sections (2 x 2 grid). In the center of the card the vocabulary term is written boldly in a circle. In the top left rectangle the students write the definition of the term. In the top right rectangle the students write characteristics of the term. In the bottom left rectangle of the card the students write examples of the term. In the bottom right rectangle of the card, students write non-examples of the term (Frayer, Frederick, & Klausmeier, 1969).
Reading Comprehension	*Sociogram*—The purpose of a sociogram is to analyze the relationships between characters in a story. Students draw circles to represent the characters in a text. The students then draw arrows between circles to show the direction of the relationship or actions between the characters. Then students write phrases or words on the arrows to describe the nature of the relationship including inferred feelings. Example: Father disapproved of Ellen. Ellen rebelled against mother (Cameron, 2004).
Writing/Point of View	*Character Diary*—The student takes on the role of a character in a story or novel and writes a diary that character might write over a specified period of time (Cameron, 2004).

Writing/Digital Literacy	*Blogging*—Students select a topic or theme and publish a blog. The blog can include visual images and text. For example, a student who enjoys horseback riding might include pictures of horses she enjoys riding, informational entries about certain techniques in horseback riding, information about riding competitions, and videos of significant events. The teacher might require specific criteria for specific entries. For example, "This week's blog entry will include an example of personification."
Figurative Language	*Song Clips*—Students pick a song they like that has clean lyrics that are appropriate for school. Then they print the lyrics to the song and get the teacher's approval. Next, students look for examples of figurative language in their songs. Students who selected the same song get into groups and compare the examples they found and see if they can uncover any others. If students selected different songs, they are placed together in a group and must decide which of the songs they selected had the best examples of figurative language. Each group shares the best one with the class.

Socially Active—What the Language Arts Experts Say

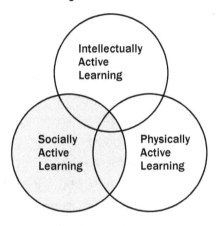

Literacy is by nature a social construct. We use reading and writing to communicate with others. Literacy is social and so are young adolescents...a perfect match. Young adolescents already engage in a social discourse to create meaning and to shape their environments through various social media outlets. Language arts teachers can help their students see the relevance of what they are learning if they can see that texts are written in social settings and for social purposes (NCTE, 2015). While it is still important to develop individual language skills in our students, we can recognize that social experiences influence the development of those skills. Middle level students can engage in talking and listening in order to explore, to connect with others, to change the world around them, and to communicate what they are learning (Finders & Hynds, 2007). Middle grades language arts teachers can capitalize on the social nature of literacy and the social nature of young adolescents by using socially active learning approaches such as literature circles, writer's workshop, and academic social networking.

Literature Circles

Day, Spiegel, McLellan, and Brown (2002) suggest that literature circles are motivating to young adolescents because frankly, talking about what you are learning is fun. Although teachers can structure literature circles in a variety of ways, the basic notion is that students gather in small groups to discuss a piece of literature in depth, preferably a novel they self-selected. There are many advantages of this small group learning method for middle grades students. If students are reading literature of interest to them, they see greater purpose in reading and learn to read more strategically with comprehension. Literature circles promote discussion because students have more opportunity to talk in small groups than in large groups, and small groups provide a more natural context for talk. These generative learning experiences also encourage responsibility and independence in young adolescents as they become more aware of their own literacy growth. Literature circles are effective in developing reading ability, knowledge about literature, and critical and analytic thinking (Parsons, Mokhtari, Yellin, & Orwig, 2011).

Book clubs, which can be very engaging to young adolescents, are another way of encouraging socially active learning. Whittingham and Huffman (2009) found that independent book clubs had a positive effect on attitudes towards reading for middle grades students who had previously been resistant to reading. The students who participated in these voluntary book clubs did so before school. The students were not required to read the same book, but rather talked about the books they were reading.

Writer's Workshop

Writer's workshop is another method of infusing socially active learning into the middle grades language arts classroom. Writer's workshop occurs over a period of time and includes time for individual writing, conferencing, and responding to the writing of peers, conferencing with the teacher, editing and revising work based on the feedback of others, and then finally, sharing and publishing of writing. The concept of writer's workshop is to simulate the work of authors and writers in the real world as it acknowledges the social nature of literacy in today's society (Finders & Hynds, 2007).

Academic Social Networking

Another method of incorporating socially active learning into the middle grades language arts classroom is academic social networking. Technologies such as wikis, blogs, Twitter, and Edmodo can motivate students to develop their communication skills and digital literacy skills in a relevant virtual environment. These tools also give middle grades language arts teachers opportunities to promote digital citizenship among their students and to teach appropriate behaviors and ethics in order to function in the modern digital world (Taranto, Dalbon, & Gaetano, 2011).

Theory into Action—Examples of Socially Active Instructional Strategies for Middle Grades Language Arts Topics

The following chart provides examples of instructional strategies that get students socially active as they explore literature and writing. The examples range across middle grades language arts topics. However, any literature can be explored through group learning, so do not limit yourself or your students.

Topic	Activity
Reading Comprehension	*Story Quilt*—Students work with partners to draw scenes and write a summary of their scene from a novel on colored paper. They place each scene on the wall like a quilt that tells the whole story of the novel. The students represent subtle ideas and themes from the text in the drawings and with their written summaries (Noe & Johnson, 1999).
Informational Literacy	*Jigsaw*—Teachers arrange students into "expert groups." Each expert group has an article related to a specific aspect of the topic. The expert groups become experts on that aspect from the article. Then the students share what they learned while in their expert groups with the members of their home groups.
Reading Fluency	*Readers' Theatre*—Students work in small groups, and the teacher gives each group a text. Students practice reading their texts and then read them aloud dramatically to the whole class. The students are expected to give a fluent and thoughtful interpretation of the text, making it engaging and comprehensible to the rest of the class.
Figurative Language	*Scavenger Hunt*—Students work in groups to find examples in a text of different literary devices. The group that finds the most items within a designated time wins a prize. For example: 1. Find an example of a hyperbole. 2. Find a metaphor. 3. Find an example of a simile. 4. Find an example of alliteration. 5. Find an example of personification. 6. Find an example of an idiom. 7. Find an example of onomatopoeia.

Text Analysis	*Highlight and Revisit*—Individually, students read a passage of text and highlight portions they think are significant. The students may highlight a word, a phrase, or an entire sentence. Next, in groups they complete a 3-column chart. In the first column they copy the exact words highlighted by someone in the group. In the second column they write the person's reason for highlighting the quote. The group then discusses the quote, and then in the third column they write new or deeper thinking that came from considering the quote (Tovani, 2004). **Quote** (record words highlighted from the text) **Reason for Highlighting** **New or Deeper Thinking**
Point of View	*To Tell the Truth*—Students prepare questions so they can interview a character from a story or novel they are reading. After they have compiled their list of questions, the teacher arranges students in small groups. A student plays the role of the character, and the other students in the group interview him or her (Finders & Hynds, 2007).
Digital Literacy	*Multimodal Learning Clubs*—Teachers assign students to a small group of students or club. Selecting a topic and meeting once a week to learn more about their topics, each club uses digital literacy strategies covered in a mini-lesson at the beginning of each club session. Once students have found sufficient information about their topic and have examined the credibility of that information, they synthesize the information into a mini-lesson for their classmates. They prepare a multimedia presentation to assist them in teaching their mini-lesson (Casey, 2012).

Physically Active—What the Language Arts Experts Say

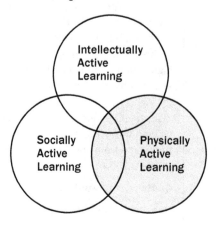

Brain research has shown that the cerebellum actually lights up when connections are made between memory and movement. In other words, if students are moving while they are learning, the brain responds. You will find that your young adolescents experience many benefits if you allow them to move a little (not all class period) during your language arts class. You will see improved understanding, improved focus, your students will view learning as fun, and will perhaps begin to see themselves as good learners (Dixon, 2013).

Multi-modal literacy projects are one example of a way to get your students up and moving while learning your language arts content. They can get out of their seats as they move around the classroom and the school to capture video clips. Drama is another good method particularly well-suited for the middle grades language arts classroom.

Examples of Physically Active Instructional Strategies

In the following chart are some examples of instructional strategies to get students physically active as they explore literature and writing across a range of middle grades language arts topics. Teachers can adapt many of these strategies for other topics as well.

Topic	Activity
Hyphens vs Dashes	*Two Corners*—One corner of the room has a card with the term *hyphen* on it. The other corner of the room has a card with *dash* written on it. The students all have a card with a sentence written on it that requires either a hyphen or a dash. The students have to figure out which corner to stand in. They can discuss their sentences together to help each other decide if they are in the correct corner. Once the students have found their respective corners, the teacher calls on students to read their sentence while other students have to determine if the student is in the correct corner and explain why or why not.
Summarizing Text	*Graffiti Wall*—This activity is used for discussion of a novel read by the whole class. Working individually or in groups, using symbols, drawings, shapes, and colors, alongside words and quotations, students construct a graphic of their section of the novel using an online tool or drawing on butcher paper with crayons or markers. When all groups have completed their graphics, they present them to the class, explaining why they chose the elements they used. Finished graphics can be displayed on a class bulletin board, on walls, or on a Web page. *http://www.readwritethink.org/classroom-resources/lesson-plans/graffiti-wall-discussing-responding-208.html*

Analogies	*Kick Me*—Students have a sheet of analogies with one word missing. The missing words are on individual slips of paper taped to students' backs. They work in partners to go around the room and look at the words on other people's backs and figure out which analogy each completes on the sheet. *https://www.teachingchannel.org/videos/ making-vocabulary-lesson-interactive*
Analyzing Text	*Beach Ball*—Process terms such as compare, contrast, describe, analyze, explain, and justify are written on a plastic beach ball. The ball is tossed to a student who is required to do the verb that his or her forefinger is pointing to, related to a character or characters in a novel. For example, "Justify Emilio's actions in the chapter," or "Describe JoAnn's emotional state in the scene."
Literature	*Character Role Play*—Students take on the role of various characters from a story, poem, or novel. The teacher asks an open-ended question that requires some inference. The students in the role of each character answer the question based on how that character might have answered it.
Analyzing Text	*Silent Discussion*—On the board, the teacher writes a question about a text the class has read. While students are working on the day's assignment, the teacher invites them one-at-a-time to write a one-sentence response to the question randomly on the board. As room allows, more than one student can write on the board at the same time, but they are not allowed to talk. Once everyone has had the opportunity, the teacher selects some of the responses to begin a whole class discussion of the question.

Multiple Topics	*Task Cards*—Instead of passing out a worksheet with practice sentences, consider cutting the sheet apart and pasting the sentences on 4 x 6 cards. Put one sentence on each card, and place the cards at stations around the room. Students may do the cards in different orders, but each student eventually rotates through all of the stations, until they have completed each sentence.

What This Looks Like in a Real Middle Grades Language Arts Classroom

Tiffany Johnson, a seventh grade language arts teacher at a rural middle school located near a military base, is a strong believer in active learning to keep her students engaged. Tiffany truly enjoys working with her students and can often be seen laughing with them. She teaches at Carver Middle School, which has a 31% minority student population that comes from various parts of the United States and the world as a result of the army base. Fifty-eight percent of the students are eligible for free or reduced lunch. I observed Tiffany teaching a lesson one morning on a novel the class was reading, *Tangerine* by Edward Bloor (2006). I have copied some excerpts from my observation notes below, and I have inserted (in italics) some of my thoughts while watching the lesson.

9:27 The lesson began with a vocabulary match activity. Tiffany distributed slips of paper. Some students had a slip with a vocabulary term and some students had a slip with a definition. All students had to find their matches. Once the students found their partners, then Tiffany got the class's attention. One-by-one each student who had a definition read their definition out loud. The rest of the class tried to guess the vocabulary term. The student with the matching term confirmed whether or not they were correct.

[This portion of the lesson involved both physically active and socially active learning.]

9:43 Tiffany told the sets of partners to find two desks beside each other. Next on the agenda was a trashball game. She asked the students questions about the novel. The questions were at different levels of challenge and were on portions of the text that they had read that week. The procedures of the game went like this: Tiffany asked a question and gave students approximately 30 seconds to 2 minutes (depending on the question) to discuss the question with their partners. Then Tiffany called a desk number at random. If the student at that desk could answer the question correctly to Tiffany's satisfaction, then one of the partners was allowed to take a shot with the trashball.

Questions Tiffany asked:

"What does Coach tell Victor to do during halftime?" (Remember level on Bloom's Taxonomy)

"Why is Paul surprised when Cara calls him?" (Understand level on Bloom's Taxonomy)

"How do you think Joey should have handled Victor when he was giving him a hard time?" (Evaluate level on Bloom's Taxonomy)

"Compare and contrast Tino and Joey. How are they alike and how are they different?" (Analysis level on Bloom's Taxonomy)

"What happens during the game since it starts so late?

How do Paul, Mom, and Dad each react?" (Remember level on Bloom's Taxonomy)

"What could all of the neighborhood's problems symbolize?" (Apply level on Bloom's Taxonomy)

"In what ways is Paul's father blind?" (Analysis level on Bloom's Taxonomy)

"What ends up in the newspaper report about the female soccer players?" (Remember level on Bloom's Taxonomy)

This is obviously a coveted game and one that is very popular with the students. Tiffany told me that she had some boys that regularly pestered her wanting her to let them play this game in just about every lesson. I couldn't help but notice how engaged the students were during the game and how hard they were trying to get the answers to the questions correct.

[This portion of the lesson would be considered intellectually active learning because the students were engaged in some higher level questioning. It would also be considered socially active because the students were working with partners. Finally, some students were allowed to be physically active if they got the opportunity to shoot the trashball.]

10:00 At this point in the lesson, Tiffany asked each group of two students to slide their desks next to another group of two students, forming new groups of four. The groups of four were told to read the novel at the point that the class left off the day before. Tiffany gave them instructions to go around the circle clockwise, with each student reading one paragraph out loud. Tiffany gave them a stopping point in the novel and told them to sit quietly once their group reached that point.

[This portion of the lesson would be considered socially

active since the students were reading the novel in small groups. However, it is not a strong example of socially active learning because the students were simply taking turns reading rather than actual collaboration.]

10:20 By this time all of the groups had reached the stopping point, and Tiffany led a whole class discussion about the selection they had just read.

Mrs. Johnson: On the bottom of page 150 Eric says, "I took in the ugliness of Joey's words, and I saw, for the first time, how different he was from me…(Bloor, 2006)" What did he mean? Dante?

Dante: They came from different families and they have different friends.

Mrs. Johnson: Yes, that's the rest of the sentence and that's true. What else did he mean? In what ways are they different?

Darius: Joey likes to pick a fight and Eric doesn't. Joey thinks Eric is a coward.

Mrs. Johnson: How do you know that? Do we have evidence from the text?

Kenya: Yeah, later he said, "You agreed to that. You'd agree to anything. Not me. I'm joining another group (Bloor, 2006)." He's saying that Eric will agree to anything just to keep others happy.

Mrs. Johnson: Do you think Eric is a coward?

Dante: No, I don't think he's a coward. He does try to avoid fighting, but I think he's just being nice to people.

Mrs. Johnson: So what does Eric mean on page 152 when he says to Joey, "Don't do this. Don't come in here with attitude (Bloor, 2006)?"

Kenya: Joey's got a bad attitude towards the kids at Tangerine Middle.

Mrs. Johnson: Why do you think he has that bad attitude?

Kenya: He wants to think he is better than they are… like he's of a better class.

Tiffany pushed them beyond the literal words of the page… she made them do some inferring and interpretation of the words of the characters.

[This portion of the lesson would be considered both intellectually active and socially active learning.]

10:28 The students rearranged the desks back to their original position and changed classes.

You, like Tiffany, can get your students engaged in active learning while they are digging into the literacy concepts that you want them to learn. You can adapt the activities listed in this chapter along with previous chapters to get your students intellectually, socially, and physically active in your language arts classroom. If you are new to active learning instructional strategies, just try one next week. Take small steps and you will soon be rewarded with engaged students who enjoy learning language arts.

Chapter 10
Active Learning in the Middle Grades Science Classroom

A good teacher inspires students to have confidence in the teacher: a great teacher inspires students to have confidence in themselves. ~Anonymous

If there is any subject in the middle grades that begs to be explored through active learning, it is science. Thinking back to my own junior high years, I find it hard to believe that my teachers reduced the learning of scientific phenomena to reading the chapter and answering the questions at the end of it. We know what we know about science because scientists have used scientific inquiry to explore the world around them. When you picture a scientist, you picture someone in a lab coat doing an experiment. The very definition of active learning!

The National Science Teachers Association (NSTA) recommends that students engage in the same behaviors as scientists—investigating the world around them through scientific inquiry. Teachers should teach students the knowledge and process skills to engage in the following:

Ask questions and define problems

Develop and use models

Plan and carry out investigations

Analyze and interpret data

Use mathematics and computational thinking

Construct explanations and design solutions

Engage in argument from evidence

Obtain, evaluate, and communicate information (NSTA, 2015b)

This can only be done in middle grades science classrooms through active learning. Lecturing via PowerPoint; reading the chapter; watching the video; and answering the questions in the workbook or worksheet, or at the end of the chapter, do not engage students in these scientific practices. Middle grades students should do scientific inquiry.

Scientific Approach

Middle grades students are capable of engaging in the exploration of science through a scientific approach, and teachers should expect this of them. Initiated by Frances Bacon in 1620, scientists have used the scientific method for centuries to uncover what we know about the natural world. Although there are different versions of the scientific method, most have these components:

Research question: Pose a specific question to be answered.

Observations: Make observations related to the question.

Hypothesis: Consider a potential explanation.

Experiment: Design an experiment to test this hypothesis.

Conclusions: Evaluate the hypothesis based on data and answer the research question.

The NSTA (2015a) endorses using a scientific approach in which middle grades students actively engage as scientists when they systematically study the physical and natural world and design and conduct experiments to investigate questions they have about that world (Herr, 2008).

Inquiry

As opposed to the teacher-directed, traditional approach to science in which the teacher or the textbook is the expert, an active learning approach involves students engaged in inquiry, and the textbook and teacher become resources. Educators often use the term inquiry loosely, but there are, indeed, different levels of inquiry. Teachers can make inquiry more or less structured and more or less open-ended depending on their comfort level and the level of their students. Wilson (2009) describes three classifications of inquiry based on the amount of guidance the teacher provides:

Open Inquiry—The teacher provides a minimal amount of guidance and structure. After the teacher gives students a general problem, students decide how to solve the problem and then locate and set up the required materials.

Guided Inquiry—The teacher provides more guidance and structure by giving the students a specific task and the materials needed to complete the task.

Directed Inquiry—The teacher provides the most guidance and structure by giving specific directions and the required materials (p. 42).

As a general rule, students need more structure at the beginning of the year. The teacher gradually removes some of that structure so students are able to successfully become more independent in their scientific investigations. It is crucial that students be intellectually, socially, and physically active in your science classroom on a regular basis.

Intellectually Active—What the Science Experts Say

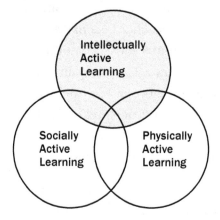

Critical Thinking

Critical thinking is the obvious goal for getting students intellectually active in science. Herr (2008) suggests some key aspects of critical thinking that are important for scientific exploration:

Identification of premises and conclusions: Critical thinkers break arguments into basic statements and draw logical implications.

Clarification of arguments: Critical thinkers locate ambiguity and vagueness in arguments and propositions.

Establishment of facts: Critical thinkers determine if the premises are reasonable and identify information that has been omitted or not collected. They determine if the implications are logical and search for potentially contradictory data.

Evaluation of logic: Critical thinkers determine if the premises support the conclusion. In deductive arguments, the conclusions must be true if the premises are true. In inductive arguments, the conclusions are likely if the premises are true.

Final evaluation: Critical thinkers weigh the evidence and arguments. Supporting data, logic, and evidence increase the weight of an argument. Contradictions and lack of evidence decrease the weight of an argument. Critical thinkers do not accept propositions if they think there is more evidence against them or if the argument is unclear, omits significant information, or has false premises or poor logic (Herr, 2008, p.125).

Analogies

One method for getting students intellectually active in science class is through analogies. Constructivist theory suggests that students learn when they make connections between what they already know and the new material. Analogies are one tool for accomplishing this because analogies make comparisons between two different things that have some similar aspects. When students make connections between the new information they are learning and something with which they are already familiar, they develop more understanding. For example, using the analogy of DNA and a spiral staircase can help students visualize the structure of DNA if they have had personal experience seeing a spiral staircase (Herr, 2008). Furthermore, asking students to make analogies themselves can challenge them intellectually. Analogies can also give insight to teachers about misconceptions that their students may have about the content (Keeley, 2008).

Modeling

Modeling is another key strategy to help students conceptually understand scientific phenomena. Having students create or explore physical models such as a model of a skeleton, a visual model such as a diagram of an electronic circuit, or an interactive 3D digital model such as one that shows the anatomy of a frog can dramatically increase their scientific knowledge and understanding (Carrejo & Reinhartz, 2014; Herr, 2008).

Theory into Action—Examples of Intellectually Active Instructional Strategies for Middle Grades Science Topics

The following chart provides examples of instructional strategies to get students intellectually active as they explore science. The examples cross a range of middle grades science topics, and many of these strategies can be adapted to fit other science topics as well.

Topic	Activity
Electricity	*Analogy*—Use plumbing as an analogy for electrical circuits. For example, relate conductive material to an open pipe and relate nonconductive material to a clogged pipe. Relate a switch to a valve, and relate voltage to water pressure. Get students started with the analogy and ask them to figure out more connections (Herr, 2008).
Plant and Animal Cells	*Venn Diagram*—Have students create a Venn diagram showing similarities and differences between plant and animal cells.
Scientific Discoveries	*Timeline*—Have students create a timeline of scientific discoveries. Ask them to look for connections between discoveries and consider what discoveries might have formed a foundation for later discoveries.
Multiple Topics	*Projects/Presentations*—Have students create a multimedia presentation using technology such as Voicethread or Prezi to explain what they have learned about a particular scientific concept.
Multiple Topics	*Concept Map*—Have students use technology such as bubbl.us or inspiration.com to create a concept map of the topic they are learning about.
Multiple Topics	*Song*—Have students create and perform a song about the concept they are studying.

Socially Active—What the Science Experts Say

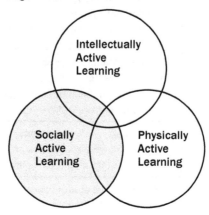

Best practices in science teaching have long included having students collaborate as they are learning science. This collaboration can take the form of partners working together, but could also include small groups of three or four students. Since scientific exploration is heavily dependent on materials and supplies that are limited or costly for schools, sometimes the amount of materials available determines the size of the groups working together. But teachers cannot let limited supplies or tools keep them from allowing their students to engage in active learning. Even if the class has only one of something, that tool can be featured in a learning station that groups of students rotate through.

One important goal of having students collaborate in science class is scientific discourse. It is important for students to question each other about the validity of their claims and for them to learn to support their claims with evidence and logical reasoning. When students complete lab experiments together, create reports about their scientific conclusions, and make presentations about what they have learned together, they are socially active.

Theory into Action—Examples of Socially Active Instructional Strategies for Middle Grades Science Topics

The following chart provides examples of instructional strategies to get students socially active as they explore science. These strategies could be adapted to learn about other middle grades science topics as well. However, any rich scientific inquiry can be done through group learning, so do not limit yourself or your students.

Topic	Activity
Organisms and Environments	*Experiment*—Give each group a live beetle and a worm. The students draw and measure the path each organism takes across a piece of paper, recording the time at equal intervals. The students then graph their data. Students can also explore the impact of light/dark environments or hot/cold environments (Tate & Phillips, 2011).
Science as a Human Endeavor	*Museum Exhibits*—Have students work in groups to create a museum exhibit. Each exhibit highlights significant discoveries of a different scientist. This can be done digitally through the 3D Gallery application on classtools.net.
Environment	*Service-Learning*—Have students create their own idea for a service-learning project that will improve their local environment. Ideas might include a recycling project, a school butterfly garden, or a koi pond for the front of the school.

Multiple Topics	*Word Sort*—Have students use the word sort strategy to examine the key vocabulary in a chapter of the textbook. Students individually select ten words or short phrases from the reading that they believe are important. After an appropriate amount of time, the students are arranged into small groups where they combine all of the word cards the students in the group wrote. They can remove any duplicate words. The group works together to arrange the cards into three or four categories and create a label for each of their categories. Next, the groups identify the five most important words from all of their cards and write one sentence using those five words to be shared with the class during the whole class discussion. The class determines if the sentences that were created are true statements based on the reading, and the accurate statements are displayed on the board for students to write in their notes (Spencer, 2008).
Multiple Topics	*Science Fairs and Science Projects*—Guide students into developing a research question related to your content. Continue to guide them as they work together in groups to answer the question. Whether you use a guided inquiry or a directed inquiry approach, allow your students to collaborate together while you provide the amount of scaffolding and support they need to be successful. Perhaps time can be devoted one day a week for students to work on their group projects over the course of several months.
Multiple Topics	*Create a Game*—Have students work together with partners or in small groups to create a game that covers the content they are currently learning.

Physically Active—What the Science Experts Say

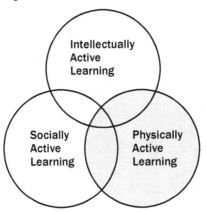

Lab experiments are the key to getting students physically active—as well as intellectually and socially active—in the classroom. Teachers must give students opportunities to touch, hold, and manipulate objects. Physical activity actually facilitates the growth of new cells in the brain as well as develops conceptual understanding of scientific phenomena (Jensen, 2008). There are numerous resources available to middle grades science teachers in which they can identify good quality lab experiments that align with their content.

One exciting method that gets students up and moving while learning scientific concepts is geospatial tools such as GPS and online mapping such as Google Earth or Virtual 3D Earth. Students can use GPS receivers to collect data that they, in turn, analyze and share with others. Students can make observations about how the physical points they have located change over time. Presentations of their analysis could include pictures they have taken of their locations (Hagevik, 2011). There are numerous other tools available to get students collecting their own data and thereby getting them up and out of their seats. Probeware, whether it is scales, accelerometers, or motion sensors, is a good example of such tools.

A promising development that has brought more active learning into middle school science classrooms is the national attention on the science, technology, engineering, and mathematics (STEM) disciplines. Many middle schools have begun implementing STEM programs that get students engaged in STEM projects such as the Toy Design Project proposed by Sirinterlikci, Zane, & Sirinterlikci (2009). Through the Toy Design Project, students use scientific inquiry to create, design, and test a new toy. Numerous STEM projects have been developed to engage students in active learning while learning science content in a manner that integrates other disciplines in an authentic way through real-world problem contexts.

Examples of Physically Active Instructional Strategies

The following chart provides examples of instructional strategies to get students physically active as they explore science. The examples cross a range of middle grades science topics, and many strategies can be adapted for other science concepts.

Topic	Activity
Inner and Outer Planets	*Smartboard*—Construct two circles on the Smartboard, one labeled inner planets and one labeled outer planets. Outside the circles place phrases and words that describe characteristics of the planets. Call on students to come to the board one-at-a-time. Each student drags one of the characteristics inside one of the circles, or moves a characteristic that a previous student placed incorrectly. The students do this without talking and while creating their own lists in two circles they have drawn in their notebooks at their desks.
Cardiovascular System	*Role-Playing*—Have students act out a blood cell traveling through the body. The students need to determine which organs are involved and students stand around the room holding cards with the names of each vessel, artery, or organ. A student plays the role of the blood cell and the class discusses what happens at each point in the cardiovascular system. A second student plays the role of carbon dioxide and is picked up along the way.
Multiple Concepts	*Sensors and Probeware*—Students can use sensors and probeware to collect data for a wide-range of experiments in physical science, earth science, and life science. Teachers can request that administrators purchase sensors for the science department such as accelerometers, barometers, motion sensors, and pH sensors. Students can ask questions and collect and analyze data using sensors and graphing skills (Herr, 2008).

Body Systems	*Learning Stations*—Have tables set up throughout the room that represent different organs or parts in a body system. The students rotate through the stations in a logical order and learn about each organ or body part at each table. For example, when studying the respiratory system, each group of students rotates through six tables: nose/mouth, pharynx, larynx, trachea, bronchi, and lungs. At each table students collect information to complete an activity sheet with a diagram of the respiratory system and details about each of the parts.
DNA	*Create a Model*—Students create a model of DNA using Twizzlers™, toothpicks, and marshmallows.
Astronomy	*Field Trip*—Take students on a field trip to a planetarium.
Ecosystems	*Nature Walk*—Walk with students around the school or to a local pond, creek, or other body of water to make observations about the local ecosystem.
Solar System	*Simulation*—Have students playing the roles of the sun, moon, and earth simulate the rotations. Have the student playing the role of the earth tilt 23.5 degrees. Have the student playing the role of the sun hold a bright light while the classroom lights are turned off and window shades are closed.

What This Looks Like in a Real Middle Grades Science Classroom

Lindsey Starnes (pseudonym), a participant in my research study, teaches seventh grade science at a suburban middle school. Seventy-three percent of the students are Caucasian, 14% are African-American, and 13% are other ethnicities.

An affluent area, only 10% of the students are on free- or reduced-lunch. Lindsey has been teaching for 25 years in a variety of middle school settings, and she has found it more and more challenging to use creative instructional methods. But she still believes strongly in the importance of using multiple learning approaches for her students to really learn the material she is teaching. I observed Lindsey one afternoon while she was teaching a lesson on genetics.

The class was an inclusion class with seven students who are identified as having special needs. The inclusion teacher was out at a meeting and was not able to be present during the class period. I excerpted some of my observation notes below, and I have also inserted (in italics) some of the thoughts I had while watching the lesson.

12:08 As students arrive in the classroom they must answer the warm-up question on the screen: "How many ways can you write the alleles for a homozygous trait? For a heterozygous trait? Give examples."

After giving the students time to write their answers, Lindsey leads a short classroom discussion and calls on several students to share their answers. She emphasizes the two vocabulary terms, *zenotype* and *genotype* and reinforces those definitions.

[This first step in the lesson is both intellectually active learning and socially active learning because students think about a higher level question and also discuss it as a class.]

12:16 The class works on their puppy project. Students clear everything off their desks except a pencil. Each group gets one blue sheet and one white sheet with detailed directions.

Lindsey tells the class: "We are going to work on the next step of our project. Look at the table on the screen. Yesterday you did the genotype and phenotype of your parent dogs. Today you are going to figure these out for the puppies of the parent dogs." Lindsey directs the students to work with their partners and create Punnett squares using the characteristics of their parent dogs. Lindsey does an example with the class first before allowing the students to go to work on their own. *As the students are working with their partners there is good energy in the room. A few students get up here and there to get materials or to ask other students questions about terms like genotypes. It is clearly acceptable to get assistance from other students as well as the teacher.*

12:30-12:45 Groups of students are working at different stages of the project. A couple of groups are using coins to determine the original traits of the parent dogs, which was the step most groups had completed the previous day. If the flipped coin is heads, it is a capital letter; if the coin is tails, it is lowercase. Some groups have finished their Punnett Squares and have begun drawing the puppies on the template they were provided.

Lindsey is all over the room monitoring every group. All of the students are engaged and everyone seems to know what they are doing and all are trying to get the task done. Very positive with the students, Lindsey is making comments such as "It looks good! Very cute!" but also uses humor with the students who make jokes about their "warped-looking puppies."

[This portion of the lesson is socially active learning because the students are working together on their puppy project.]

12:47 Lindsey tells the students to put their dogs in a Ziploc bag and clean up their materials.

12:50 Lindsey debriefs the class about the puppy activity which will be completed the next day. She reinforces the unit vocabulary by asking several questions such as:

What is another word for homozygous?

What is another way to say phenotype?

What is another way to say heterozygous?

12:57 The class is dismissed.

You, like Lindsey, can get your students engaged in active learning while they are digging into the science concepts that you want them to learn. You can adapt the activities listed in this chapter along with previous chapters to get your students intellectually, socially, and physically active in your science classroom. If you are new to active learning instructional strategies, then just try one next week. Take small steps and you will soon be rewarded with engaged students who enjoy learning science.

Chapter 11

Active Learning in the Social Studies Classroom

If we succeed in giving the love of learning, the learning itself is sure to follow. ~John Lubbock

The National Council for the Social Studies (NCSS) (2010) recommends 10 thematic strands that should run throughout social studies instruction:

- Culture
- Time, continuity, and change
- People, places, and environments
- Individual development and identity
- Individuals, groups, and institutions
- Power, authority, and governance
- Production, distribution, and consumption
- Science, technology, and society
- Global connections
- Civic ideals and practices

The organization has also identified skills that students should acquire in order to make sense of the ten social studies themes:

- Data-gathering skills
- Intellectual skills
- Decision-making skills
- Interpersonal skills

They suggest, as do other social studies experts, that the abilities to research, analyze, synthesize, interpret, and evaluate information are important for students to think critically about the world in which they live. They can gain these abilities by active learning.

Schmidt (2007) argues that we have lost the "social" in social studies and that social studies should be about the

> "human interest, heartbreak, adventure, conflict, invention, competition, disappointment, treachery, heroism, strategic brilliance, and spectacular foibles that allow kids to discover what they have in common with people who lived in other places, times, and cultures." (p. 3)

She suggests putting the social back in social studies in three ways. First, we can put the social into the content by focusing on people, their trials and challenges, as well as their triumphs over time. History should not be a series of dates and events, but the stories of people and how they were impacted by the world around them. Second, we can put the social into the learning by using instructional practices that are natural for human beings such as "talking, observing, modeling, collaborating, sensing, responding emotionally, and having physical experiences in their environment." (p. 7)

Third, we can put the social into the outcomes by encouraging students to take action based on what they learn and empowering them to get involved in solving real-world problems.

Intellectually Active—What the Social Studies Experts Say

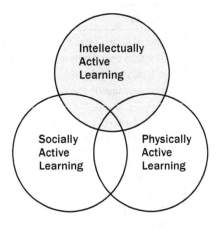

Students must be intellectually active to develop the data-gathering, intellectual, decision-making, and interpersonal skills recommended by NCSS. In middle grades social studies classes, students should be involved in researching topics across the ten themes on a regular basis. To push students to think critically, teachers should teach them the skills to acquire information using a variety of technologies and resources and to analyze, synthesize, interpret, and evaluate that information. It is also important for teachers to create opportunities for students to create informative and creative presentations to share what they have learned with their classmates (Melber & Hunter, 2010).

Theory into Action—Examples of Intellectually Active Instructional Strategies for Middle Grades Social Studies Topics

The following chart provides examples of instructional strategies for getting students intellectually active as they explore social studies. The examples cross a range of middle grades social studies topics and teachers easily can adapt many of the strategies to fit other social studies topics as well.

Topic	Activity
Culture	*Cultural Game*—Have students research a culture as they learn about games played in it. Each student (or group of students) selects one game and learns the rules for playing the game. Using the game, the student then designs a review game of the content the class is studying. The whole class plays the game (Tate, 2012).
Synthesis	*Picture Graphic Organizer*—Have students draw a picture related to the content the class is studying and then have them turn that picture into a graphic organizer about the content (Tate, 2012).
Intellectual Skills	*Metaphors*—Have students make connections between two unlike concepts. For example: How is America like a salad bowl? How is democracy like a railway station? How is an election like a pizza (Tate, 2012)?
People, Places, and Environments	*Glogster*—Have students create Glogsters (electronic posters) about a topic. The Glogster could be about a historical figure, a country, a culture, a religion, or an issue.

Global Connections	*Global Pen Pals*—Find a teacher in a country the class is studying who is willing to allow his or her students to be pen pals via email with your students. Assign all students pen pals from the other country. The pen pals will exchange a series of emails throughout the year on topics teachers agree upon. The emails could focus on the structure of the government, economic issues, or cultural traditions, for example.	
Conflicts in American History	*Curating an Exhibit*—Have students create a museum exhibit by selecting from given artifacts such as letters and paintings according to a theme of their choosing. They write descriptors for each artifact in their exhibit. Examples of themes are change, conflict, exploration, aspirations, globalization, or poverty. Classtools. net has a 3D Gallery tool that allows students to create a museum exhibit digitally.	
Global Issues	*Option Display*—Have students try to generate options for solving a problem through research on the Internet and interviews with whoever might be helpful. Creating a display that explains the problem, they show several options for solutions, the possible consequences of each option, and the recommendation for the best option. Examples of problems are:	
	What might reduce prejudice? How might we help the poor? What can we do to fix immigration issues? How can we get more people voting in elections? (Harmin, 1995)	
	Students can structure their display like this:	
	Explanation of the problem	
	List of three or more possible options for handling the problem.	Chief advantages and disadvantages of each option.
	Overall recommendation	

Socially Active—What the Social Studies Experts Say

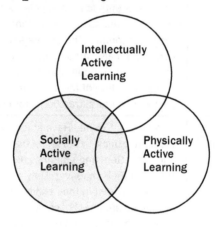

It seems intuitive that having middle grades students be socially active during their social studies class would put the "social" in social studies. As future citizens engaged in a democracy, students must learn to dialogue with others who have different perspectives (NCSS, 2010). Young adolescents must talk about what they are learning and grapple together over the many complex issues in our world. Collaborative, project-based instruction is an ideal method to accomplish this, especially if students can conduct oral interviews of diverse people in those projects (Melber & Hunter, 2010). Hernandez-Ramos and De La Paz (2009) found that middle grades students who were engaged in project-based learning made significantly more gains in content knowledge than students who experienced more traditional learning.

Theory into Action—Examples of Socially Active Instructional Strategies for Middle Grades Social Studies Topics

In the following chart are examples of instructional strategies to get students socially active as they explore social studies. The examples range across middle grades social studies topics. However, students can work on any rich historical topic in groups, so do not limit your classes to these topics.

Topic	Activity
Introducing a Country	*Tour Guides*—Put the students into groups and assign each group a country. Each group plans a field trip for the rest of the class to that country and virtually takes the class there. Challenge students to be creative in presenting information about the country and its culture. When a group finishes their presentation, the rest of the class should feel as if they actually had gone to the country (Tate, 2012).
Culture	*Presentations*–Assign students to small groups and give each small group a world culture to explore. Students prepare presentations about the behaviors, beliefs, traditions, values, institutions, and ways of living of that culture (Tate, 2012).
Historical Events	*News Broadcast*—Have students work in small groups to prepare a news broadcast. This could be a broadcast that might have happened on the evening of a historical event or about a historical figure or about current events in a region or country. Two members of the group can play the role of the on-set anchors and two members of the group can play the role of on-the-scene reporters (Tate, 2012).

Global Connections	*Animoto Presentation*—Arrange students into groups and assign each group a global issue such as poverty, terrorism, or health care. Each group researches the issues and solutions that have been tried and prepares an Animoto presentation on their issue for the class. *www.animoto.com*
Global Issues	*NGO Presentation*—Have students research social and environmental problems and brainstorm solutions. The teacher plays the role of a generous benefactor who has 5 billion dollars to distribute to non-governmental organizations (NGOs). The students work in groups, with each group representing their own NGO, which they name. The NGO must have a focus issue, focus region, and solution. Each NGO group creates a Prezi presentation with a proposal for funding their solution. In this presentation they explain the problem, present their solution, justify the funding needed and explain the urgency of the funding (Debbink, 2008).
Data-Gathering Skills	*Primary Source Scavenger Hunt*—Have students work in small groups to research everything they can about a specific event, period of time, culture, or person using only primary documents. Examples of primary documents are: arrest records, advertisements, catalogues, censuses, laws, ledgers, newspapers, recipes, and wills. Students share their discoveries by creating a Glogster on the topic.
Constitution	*Supreme Court Trial Simulation*—Have students act out a Supreme Court case and make arguments about a constitutional amendment that is selected. Assign students to groups and each group is given a supreme court case to study related to that amendment. Arrange the room to look like a courtroom and assign students roles to play: justices, attorneys for the petitioner, attorneys for the respondents, etc. The students act out the trials, and the justices summarize the decisions that the real supreme court made (DiCamillo & Gradwell, 2012).

Physically Active—What the Social Studies Experts Say

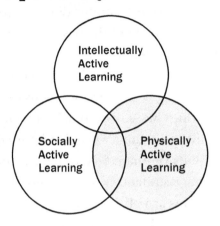

One of the many possibilities for getting students physically active while learning social studies actually gets them out of the classroom. Field trips are ideal ways to provide students with authentic experiences that bring relevance to the content (Melber & Hunter, 2010; Sprenger, 2007). Local and state government offices are an obvious possibility as well as the local chamber of commerce. Museums typically offer educational experiences that include historical reenactments (Van Scotter, White, Hartoonian & Davis, 2007). In addition to museums and government agencies, many other sites in the local community allow students a deeper level of engagement with the content.

Another common strategy to get students physically active in the social studies classroom is to have them make a physical model. Physical models or dioramas related to an event or concept can aid students in mental processing of information (Marzano, 2007).

A third method for getting students physically active in the classroom, simulations, is particularly ideal for the subject of social studies. Melber and Hunter (2010) argue that one way historians learn about the past is through careful reconstruction of it. Role-playing a real-life situation can help students learn about the events and make sense of the context and issues surrounding it. These simulations can enhance students' critical thinking skills and help students make sense of the everyday lives of ordinary people who lived through extraordinary events (Putnam & Rommel-Esham, 2004). Teachers can engage students in simulations of things other than historical events as well (Gregory & Herndon, 2010). For example, DiCamillo and Gradwell (2012) observed two eighth grade social studies teachers as their classes participated in simulations of Supreme Court trials and immigrants arriving at Ellis Island. Assessment data showed that those students made learning gains and were able to understand the issues that were explored through role-play.

Examples of Physically Active Instructional Strategies

The following chart provides instructional strategies to get students physically active as they explore social studies. The examples range across middle grades social studies topics and teachers can adapt the strategies for other topics as well.

Topic	Activity
Historical Events or People	*Role Playing*—Have students take on the persona of a significant figure or have a group of students reenact a historical event.
How a Bill Becomes a Law	*Field Trip*—Take students to the state capitol to meet with a legislator or observe a legislative session.
People, Places, and Environments	*Charades*—Give a student a card with a vocabulary term, historical event, or historical character written on the card. The student acts out what is on the card without speaking. The first student in the class to guess correctly gets a point. The student who accumulates the most points by the end of the game, wins (Tate, 2012).
Historical Events	*Diorama*—Have students create a diorama or physical model of a historical event or other concept.
Time, Continuity, and Change	*Artifact Hunt*—Place artifacts around the room from a period in history or from a region or country in the world. Students walk around the room and examine each artifact. They record on a sheet what they think the artifact is and what it might be used for (Tate, 2012).
Geography	*Plaster of Paris Map*—Students create a physical map of a country or region using plaster of Paris to represent various geographical features.

Branches of the Federal Government	*Graphic Organizer*—Put three posters around the room labeled executive, legislative, and judicial. Give each student a sticky note with a governmental role on it such as senator, supreme court justice, or vice president. At a designated time, students move to the poster with the branch of government they would work in. Once the students are at the correct poster, the students at that poster should arrange their sticky notes on the poster to create a graphic organizer showing the relationships between the different roles of government officials in that branch of government (Tate, 2012).
Time, Continuity, and Change	*Living Time Line*—Give students cards with historical events written on them. The students with cards have to arrange themselves in a line in the front of the room in order, while the remaining students at their seats tell them which order to get in. (Tate, 2012).

What This Looks Like in a Real Middle Grades Social Studies Classroom

Sofia Martinez (pseudonym), a participant in my research study, teaches sixth grade social studies at Timberwood Middle School, which is a rural school with a population that is approximately 50% African-American and 50% Caucasian. Seventy-one percent of the students are on free or reduced lunch. Sofia is a risk taker who does not mind trying new things in the classroom. Constantly on the lookout for a new method to reach her students, she gets ideas from other teachers, from professional development sessions, and from the Internet. She is good at taking a nugget of an idea from somewhere and adapting it to fit what she wants to do in her lesson. When you are in her classroom, you cannot help noticing that she really likes her students and they really like her. I observed Sofia teaching a lesson about the gross domestic product as part of an economics unit. Following are excerpts from my observation notes with inserts (in italics) of my thoughts while watching the lesson.

12:05 The students came into the classroom from lunch and got settled. There was a warm-up on the screen that said, "Study p. 22-23 for a few minutes. Quiz coming right up!" Sofia told everyone to clear their desks except for a Playdoh® container and a writing utensil. She passed out the quiz, which consisted of six multiple choice questions and told students to begin kneading their Playdoh® after finishing the quiz.

12:20 Sophia tells the students, "Put the lid on your container and set it aside. Hide your pen or pencil. You will not be able to use either today." She makes them put their hands in their laps to stop playing with Playdoh®. "Today we are going to learn about the GDP. We are going to pretend we are the Martinez Country. Each of you represents a factory. We are going to simulate the things that will be produced in Martinez Country. We will look at three years of data to see how our GDP changes. Playdoh® is one of your resources. It is capital that you are going to spend to make something else. The container is not a tool that is available to you." Sophia asked students what other capital they could use and students suggested answers such as the desk, the school building, and their hands.

I noticed that none of the students thought it at all unusual that they were making things with Playdoh® in their sixth grade social studies class. I got the impression that the students are used to a variety of things happening in this classroom—it is just the normal course of doing business.

12:25 "In round one, the year 2012, you are responsible for producing two items." The students selected items from a list on the board. "As your supervisor, if I walk around and see that you are not making a quality product I am going to tell you to start over. We have to produce quality merchandise to distribute."

Sophia instructed them to start and the students all began making their products. No one was talking. Everyone was on task.

[This portion of the lesson is physically active learning.]

12:30 "How many of you made only one item? If you were in a command economy and you didn't make your quota, you would probably be sent home." Sophia had the students raise their hands to tally how many made which items on a chart in the front of the room. She explained that she was checking their production for year one.

12:35 Sophia told the students to knead (destroy) the products they had just made, and then said

"For 2013, you get to make one item that you already produced, but you only have 3 minutes. It is called specialization. It needs to be a good quality product."

I noticed throughout the lesson that Sophia was continually using economic terminology. She also inserted humor throughout the lesson. It was obvious that the students were used to this and responded well to it.

[This portion of the lesson is physically active learning.]

12:38 Sophia asked the students how many thought they had made the product better the second time. "That is specialization. You concentrate on one thing and do it really well."

Sophia discussed the value of products and that value is what a product is worth, not necessarily its price at Wal-Mart. She gave each item on the list on the board a value and the class calculated the revenue for each item and the GDP for the entire column. The class agreed that the GDP decreased from 2012 to 2014. Sophia asked the students what would make a GDP go down. The class discussion that ensued included points such as service jobs versus goods-oriented jobs and the environment ("If there wasn't much rain, it could affect our resources"). One student suggested price. Sophia explained how the price didn't impact GDP—it came down to its worth. She clarified that GDP is the value of goods.

Sophia's interactions with the students were positive; they obviously like her and are responding well to her. None of the students resisted any of the things she asked them to do. The climate of the classroom was one of energy.

[This portion of the lesson is socially active learning.]

12:55 "You have three minutes to make as many of whatever items you want. Some of you will get paid the value of whatever items you make."

As they were working, Sophia called some students to the front and gave them play money.

She gave one student the option of spending some of her money to invest in a new tool (cookie cutter) to make more of her product (butterflies) the next time.

[This portion of the lesson is physically active learning.]

1:05 The bell rang and the students left to go to their next class.

You, like Sophia, can get your students engaged in active learning while they are digging into the social studies concepts that you want them to learn. You can adapt the activities listed in this chapter along with previous chapters to get your students intellectually, socially, and physically active in your classroom. If you are new to active learning instructional strategies, then just try one next week. Take small steps and you will soon be rewarded with engaged students who enjoy learning social studies.

Part Four

Introduction
Overcoming Challenges and Barriers

As you have been reading this book there might have been a time or two that you said to yourself, "That's nice, but..." or "I agree with this in theory, but..." or "I wish I could do these strategies, but..." I get that. I have been there. I understand. Teaching middle school is an extremely difficult thing and implementing active learning is even harder. Teachers face many challenges when trying to incorporate active learning. The next two chapters will explore the most common ones and provide ideas for overcoming those challenges. But the bottom line is this: Yes, the challenges are there. Yes, this is hard. But is it worth it? Yes. Your students will be much more engaged, and their learning will increase dramatically when you meet the challenges and make it happen.

Chapter 12
Overcoming the "Kids Can't Handle It" Issue

Our aim is to discipline for activity, for work, for good,
not for immobility, not for passivity, not for obedience.
~Maria Montessori

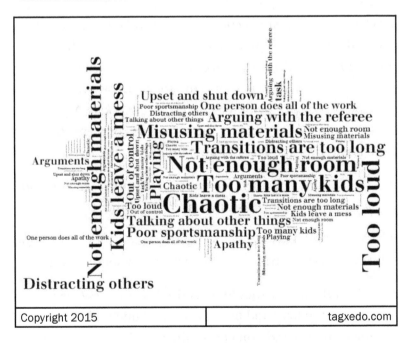

Copyright 2015	tagxedo.com

This chapter explains workable classroom management and organization strategies that help teachers work with 30 kids and get them on task and engaged in active learning. When teachers hear about ideas for active learning, a common thought that goes through their minds is "Will I be able to keep the students under control?" Visions of chaos dance in our minds. Ironically, active learning actually gets more of the students engaged more of the time. The goal of this chapter is to increase teachers' comfort level in managing their students during active learning by offering a variety of strategies.

Barriers

When I talk with teachers about active learning, most teachers respond positively. They understand it is developmentally appropriate for young adolescents and think it key to helping them become critical thinkers. Basically, they are sold on the idea...but...There is always a "but" afterwards and it goes something like this, "I can see how active learning would work in some classrooms in other schools where they have perfect children, *but* you haven't met *my kids*. My kids can't handle it." See if any of these specific concerns that I have heard over the years sound familiar.

- "Yes, I think it is good for students to work in groups, *but my kids* will get off task and talk about other things."

- "Yes I think kids should do hands-on activities, *but my kids* take forever to transition and we waste a lot of class time."

- "Yes, I think kids should do active learning, *but my kids* just get too loud and out of control. And besides they make messes and don't clean them up."

- "Yes, I think kids should work together when they are learning, *but my kids* start arguing."

- "Yes, I think kids should have physical movement during a lesson, *but my kids* get out of control."

- "Yes, I think kids should work in groups, *but my kids* will sit back and let one student do all of the work."

Okay, I hear you. And I have to tell you something. Your kids sound just like my kids. I have worked in a variety of middle grades classrooms—urban, rural, and suburban. I have observed middle school teachers in a variety of classrooms. I have interacted with literally thousands of middle grades students. Those perfect children in other schools and other teachers' classrooms? Actually, they don't exist. The elephant in the room that we all need to acknowledge is that middle grades students misbehave, doing things that they are not supposed to and failing to do things they are supposed to do. Their pre-frontal cortex is not fully developed and it shows.

However, something else to consider is that middle grades students also will misbehave during passive learning instructional strategies. Any teacher who believes that every student was on task throughout her entire lecture is just fooling herself. Yes, students will get off task during small group activities, but they also get off task during lectures and when doing worksheets. They just do it mentally, so it is not as disruptive. But the result is the same. Learning does not happen.

So no, this chapter is not the magic pill that promises if you follow these strategies you will suddenly have perfect, well-behaved, engaged students. However, these strategies will help you manage their behavior and get more of them engaged more of the time.

Possible Solutions

Yes it is tough, but it is worth the effort. The first step is finding teachers who excel at managing their classrooms while incorporating active learning and asking them how they do it. No matter what grade level or subject they teach, other teachers can borrow good ideas from them. There is an old saying that, "Those who think it can't be done should get out of the way of those who are doing it". One year my third period was a very challenging group—the bane of my existence. It didn't take much for them to spin out of control. I blamed it on a bad mix of kids that just pushed each other's buttons. One day I had a dentist appointment and left during second period when the substitute arrived. As I was walking down the hall to my car, I saw my third period group in Mrs. Bratton's classroom. Perfect angels. They were all sitting quietly looking at her, several had their hands raised, eager to answer whatever question she was asking. I could not believe my eyes. I figured she must be bribing them with something, and I had witnessed some kind of fluke. A few days later, I was out in the hall again during second period and amazingly, saw a similar scenario when I peeked into Mrs. Bratton's classroom. Impossible coincidence. I had to begin to admit to myself that it was possible for that group of students to behave and that if Mrs. Bratton was capable of controlling them, then I should be able to as well. I began my quest to learn from her. I guarantee that there is at least one teacher at your school that is able to do active learning with students that are as challenging as yours. Seek them out, ask them questions, observe them teach, have them observe you and give you advice. You will be glad you did.

The following sections describe strategies for effectively managing the chaos. Some may work well in your present classroom management system and may enhance what you are already doing. Managing students during active learning often requires adding techniques and effort beyond the normal classroom management structure. Feel free to try some or all of these ideas and adapt them to make them work for you and your students.

Engaging Lesson Plan

Although it may be counterintuitive, the best way to get students to behave is to incorporate active learning into your lesson plan. It may seem logical that adding an activity that requires movement or group work or hands-on materials will cause students to get off task and out of control. It may also seem logical to think that students are easier to control when they work individually sitting quietly in rows of desks. In reality, the opposite is true. If students can do something interesting that requires them to be actively engaged, most (maybe not all) will naturally behave. If most of the students are behaving and engaged, then you can focus on the few who are not. Frankly, middle grades students spend much of their day doing passive learning and when they are presented with something different, anything different, they are intrigued. An exciting, engaging lesson plan is the first step for managing students' behavior. When writing your lesson plans, see how you can get the students actively involved. Start small. Even just one short active learning strategy can enhance a lesson plan.

Ease into It

If you or your students do not have a lot of experience with active learning, then ease into it. The first activity of the first week of school need not involve groups with students doing physical movement and using lots of hands-on materials with a really challenging question. The lesson will crash and burn, and you only will be discouraged. Ease into it. On the first few days of the school year, keep things really calm until you feel like you have general control of the classroom and have begun getting into the routine of your normal classroom procedures. When you introduce the first active learning strategy, just introduce one aspect. For example, the first time you do socially active learning, use partners (not groups) and let the activity be a very short one. If the class is successful with that, then you might do a longer activity the next time or you might do groups of three. You can gradually work up to groups of four. If they are able to work in groups successfully, then you can incorporate some physical movement or a hands-on activity. Do not be in a hurry to do too much too quick. Ease into it and build on success.

Use Active Learning as Leverage

It is very effective to use active learning as leverage in maintaining student behavior. It goes something like this, "We will do this really fun activity as long as you are on task and working hard...if you do not do what you are supposed to, then we will do this other extremely boring, horrible worksheet that I have prepared for you." Maybe you won't use those exact words but you get the gist. You are letting them know that the activity will require them to think and work hard but it will be fun and worth the effort. Make the learning the reward. It works. They are tired of the boring worksheets…they have seen enough of those and will stay within your parameters in order to do the more interesting activity.

The key here is consistency. Always have an alternative assignment in your back pocket that you can pull out if needed. It might be a page in a workbook or the textbook. Or it might be a worksheet. Whatever type of assignment it is, it should cover the same skill or concept as the planned activity, just in a less interesting manner. If an individual student, a small group of students, or a whole class of students does not handle the active learning strategy appropriately, then they do the alternative assignment on their own.

Although you will not like giving the alternative assignment to an individual student or a class, you will find that sacrificing one or two activities makes the point and enables your students to successfully complete the many others that they will do the remaining 178 days of the year.

Word on the Board

This is absolutely the most effective management strategy for active learning. The teacher selects a word, it could be the school mascot, the teacher's last name, the name of the subject, or a vocabulary term. Always use the same word. When the students get too loud or a little out of hand, simply walk to the board and begin spelling the word on the board. If you are on the opposite side of the room, you may sometimes choose to spell it verbally. Begin spelling the word slowly and continue writing letters until the class gets quiet. When everyone is quiet, then stop spelling and remind them to stay calm and to keep the noise level at an appropriate volume. Everyone can then get back to work. If the class gets too loud again, then pick up with the last letter spelled and continue spelling until they are quiet again. As long as you do not spell the entire word before the end of the class period, everything is fine. But if you do get to the final letter, the class stops whatever activity it is doing immediately and for the remainder of that class period and for the entire following day, the class does the most boring assignment you can find. Of course, you will want to explain how and why you will be using this strategy before you do it for the first time.

The beauty of this strategy is that it gives middle grades students wiggle room. They are not going to be perfect and, frankly, sometimes they get really excited about a game or an activity and they forget to keep their voices down. This strategy allows enough room for them to not be perfect, but it does have a clear line so that they cannot continue being too loud. If you are firm and consistent, it works really well. If they know you will follow through, they will do what they have to do to be able to participate in active learning as opposed to more worksheets.

Too Noisy App

The Too Noisy App, *http://toonoisyapp.com*, is a noise level meter with a dial that moves according to the volume of noise in the room. The teacher can set the sensitivity of the meter to whatever level is considered loud enough for students who are talking as they work together on an activity. If the noise level gets beyond the point set by the teacher, the app will sound an alarm. The dial ranges from green to yellow to red, so everyone in the room can see when the volume is approaching the too noisy level. As a teacher, you can decide the consequences if the too noisy alarm goes off. If you want to pair this strategy with the word on the board strategy, it could just be that when the too noisy alarm goes off, you add letters to the word.

Over Plan

An important method to keeping everything under control while doing active learning in a middle grades classroom is to over plan ahead of time. Think through the logistics of the lesson before the class and try to predict where potential problems could occur. Organize the activity as much as possible, especially for your first several attempts. Write activity directions on a handout as well as saying them verbally. If students will work in groups, go ahead and decide who will work with whom and how they get that information and transition to the group. Color coding can often be helpful with organization. Have materials ready ahead of time and devise an efficient system for distributing them. Having students responsible for distributing and cleaning up materials is usually the best approach. Have a materials organization system. For example, having labeled containers for materials that are located in a particular space in the classroom allows students to get the materials they need as they need them. But be clear that it is their responsibility to ensure that the materials are returned to the appropriate containers by the end of the period. It is a good practice to always allow the last two minutes of class time for students to clean up their areas. Students are generally more compliant in putting away materials if they are not worried about being tardy to the next class.

More Structure Rather than Less

Especially in the beginning, middle grades students need more structure rather than less. As the year goes on and you get more comfortable, you can give students more and more independence. There are different ways you can give students more structure. One is time limits. Break the activity into chunks and set a time limit for each chunk. Display a timer. Begin with 5- to 10-minute chunks and extend the time as the year goes on and as the students can handle it. For example, you might tell students that they must select a topic by 11:50, or they must have at least three pieces of information about the topic written on their sheet by 12:00.

Another method for adding structure is specifying resources and places to get information. For example, instead of telling students to go research a topic, send them to specific sites with specific questions. As the year goes on, allow them to come up with their own questions and determine the best place to get the information they need. The activity itself can have more or less structure depending on how many directions you supply on the paper. It is important to give middle grades students more and more independence in making decisions for themselves. Reward them for making wise decisions and continually remind them of the value of being able to figure things out on their own.

Clear Directions

Many attempts at active learning fall apart not because the students are unwilling or uncooperative, but because the students are just confused about what they are supposed to be doing. Make your directions as clear as possible. Explain directions, one step at a time. Pair oral and written directions. Ask students questions about the directions you just gave or have a student paraphrase what you just asked the class to do. Give students an opportunity to ask questions about the directions. What seems obvious to you may not be so obvious to every student. We all sometimes have a tendency to leave out a critical piece of information because we assume everyone already knows it. If the students understand what they are supposed to do, most (maybe not all) students will attempt to follow those directions. If most of the students are following your directions, then you can focus on the few that are lost (or wandering), rather than having the whole class dissolve into chaos.

Head It Off at the Pass

Try to predict the potential problems. What part of this activity will be tempting for middle grades students to disrupt? Address that point specifically when going over your directions and establish a clear expectation. For example, always begin an activity that involves meter sticks by first reminding students that meter sticks are for measurement purposes only and not for sword fighting. Say it in a humorous way, but make sure the students know that you expect them to use the tools appropriately. Middle graders are often surprised that you can read their minds, not knowing how many times you have seen the very actions they are plotting.

Do an Example Together

Depending on the activity, you might consider doing an example problem together or displaying what an appropriate response, product, or outcome might look like. Sometimes, students just need a vision of where they are headed in order to get started. You might begin the first step of an activity together as a class and then let them continue in their groups. Often, the trick is to just get them started and allow their momentum to take them the rest of the way. Again, this is a method of scaffolding that you will want to remove as the year goes on. The goal is for the students to develop the ability to be self-starters and to be as independent as possible in their learning.

Gotchas

Getting students truly active intellectually is one of the most challenging aspects of teaching middle grades if not the most challenging. Thinking is hard work and young adolescents are not the only people who avoid exercising their brain muscle. However, many middle grades teachers get all types of learners actively engaged in intellectual activity through a variety of instructional approaches.

A strategy that you may find helpful in motivating your students to think more deeply is a token system called "Gotchas." The tokens are little slips of paper with the word "Gotcha" printed on them. If a student answers a particularly challenging question or takes an intellectual risk they earn a gotcha. As in positive behavior systems, students can trade gotchas for rewards such as homework passes or choosing where to sit during class. But unlike positive behavior systems, gotchas are not earned for good behavior, they are earned for good thinking.

Timer

Transitions can be problematic due to middle grades students' tendency to dawdle if given some freedom in the classroom. One way to make transitions go more smoothly is to display a timer. Give the students an appropriate amount of time to get the materials they need, get into their groups, and begin the task. Any student who is not in his or her seat and working when the timer goes off is removed from the group and given the alternative assignment to work on alone. If you are consistent with this, they will quickly figure out how to get there in time. Hold up your alternative assignment while giving them directions to make the point that you have a boring worksheet ready and you are not afraid to use it. The students have no trouble believing it is true. It is also a good idea to pair a reward with this strategy. If everyone is in their place and working when the timer goes off, then a marble goes in the jar. When the jar is full, the class gets a reward such as a popcorn party.

10- to 15-Minute Rule

It is the rare activity that will keep middle grades students engaged and focused for more than 10-15 minutes, so it is important to break up lessons into 10- to 15-minute chunks. For example, if you have an activity that will take the students approximately 30 minutes to complete, break it up into part A and part B. Give the students 15 minutes to complete part A and then bring the class together as a whole to discuss that part. Once the whole class discussion is finished, then the students go back to their groups to work on part B. You will find that you are able to keep your students' attention and keep them focused more effectively if you work in 10- to 15-minute chunks. As students can handle it, you can extend this sometimes so it is not a hard-and-fast rule, but it is a rule that will serve you well.

Have a Signal

Whenever students are allowed to talk in the classroom, whether they are working in small groups or playing a game, there will be noise. At some point, you will need to get their attention—to move to the next activity or to end the current one, to give them new directions or to clarify the directions you already gave, or to regulate the noise level. Whatever the reason, it works to have a signal that is agreed upon ahead of time. The students know that when they hear the signal, they are to get quiet and look at you for further information. Some ideas for signals are: a rainstick, a bell chime, a clapping rhythm, or some kind of chant. I strongly suggest you have something other than, "Let me have your attention" or "Listen up". Relying on your voice to give them direction will lose effectiveness over time. As time goes by, you will find yourself yelling louder and repeating it more often. A signal is more effective, and it is important that you enforce the signal. If a student ignores the signal and just keeps talking, then give them the alternative assignment and remove them from the group.

Return to Individual Seats

Usually, when students work in small groups, there is a point the class comes together to wrap up. Students may have been working on an interesting problem or question and you will next lead a whole class discussion about what they learned. Or perhaps you want to confirm that everyone understood part A of the activity before you give directions and move on to part B. Having students sitting in small groups can sometimes be counterproductive to a whole class discussion. Because students are encouraged to talk and work together when in small groups, they naturally and subconsciously think it is fine to talk when they are seated in small groups. It is not automatic for students to switch gears to a whole class discussion in which one person in the classroom speaks at a time. Some students will attempt to continue sidebar conversations with their group members. It is easy to distinguish between small groups (where students are allowed to talk freely) and whole class discussions (where only one person should speak at a time), if you simply have students leave their small groups and go back to their original individual seats for the whole class discussion (Edwards, 2011).

Chart Paper and Accountability

One method of keeping students on task is to have accountability measures built in that give students a reason to accomplish what you have asked them to do. And no, this does not mean that you grade everything. If you have students working in small groups, give the groups chart paper during exploration activities to record their thinking so that it can be shared with the class later. When students know that they are going to have to share what they learned with the class, it helps keep them focused during the small group exploration time. Other methods for recording thinking are: pens on clean paper that can be displayed on a document camera, a large dry-erase board that is big enough for all group members to work on and can be seen from across the room, or electronic tablets or other devices. The point is that students have to display what they did in front of the class.

Check in with All Groups First

A helpful strategy in managing students working in small groups is to check in with all of the groups in the class to get them started before helping a particular group that is having trouble. Always follow the same general process when getting students to work in groups. First, go over the expectations and directions of the activity. Next, ask a student to paraphrase the directions and ask the class a couple questions about what might be confusing in the directions. Go over behavior expectations unique to the activity (e.g., "We will not be doing sword fighting with the yardsticks"). Then give students a reasonable amount of time to get whatever materials they may need and to move their desks into their groups. Let them know that if they are not working by the time the timer goes off, they will be working individually. Next, walk around and check in with every group. Make sure everyone is getting started and seems to understand their task at hand. After you have checked in with every group and everyone seems to be working, you will begin going to individual groups who are asking for assistance.

Self-Select Groups

At times you will want to assign students to groups for various reasons. You may want to group students homogeneously so that you can differentiate their assignment, to separate students who misbehave when they are together, or to group students heterogeneously for a given activity. Surprisingly, from a management standpoint, sometimes it is easiest to control students when they self-select their groups. Using this as leverage goes something like this, "If you work hard and remain on task, I will allow you to select with whom you work. However, if you do not work as you should, then you will be working by yourself."

Harmin (1995) suggests two advantages of allowing students to self-select their groups occasionally. First, it is efficient. The teacher avoids taking the time to create the list of group assignments and just tells the students to get into groups. Secondly, self-selection helps students learn how to take initiative in social situations. It is likely you will also observe less arguing in groups that are self-selected.

Though it is not a good idea always for students to self-select their groups, it makes management a lot easier because students will behave to gain the privilege of working with their friends.

Co-teaching Strategies

If you happen to have an inclusion class or a situation where two teachers are assigned to co-teach, Friend and Bursuck (2012) offer co-teaching strategies that work well for active learning.

Station Teaching—In station teaching the students rotate through learning stations in small groups, with each of the teachers leading a station. Because each station can meet the needs of a particular group of students, this works well for differentiation. It also works well for active learning because the teachers can be leading the stations that require more active learning, while the stations that students do independently can be calmer, more passive learning approaches. If each teacher works with a small group of students, together they can more easily manage behavior as students engage in activities, rather than one teacher trying to manage an entire class doing that same activity.

Parallel Teaching—In parallel teaching, teachers divide the class into two groups, and each group works with one of the teachers. Again, this is ideal for active learning, because one of the teachers can be working with half the class using a passive learning approach, while the other teacher works with half of the class using an active learning approach. It is easier to manage half of a class doing an activity, rather than managing the entire class.

Alternative Teaching—In alternative teaching one teacher leads the majority of the class, while the second teacher leads a small group in an alternative activity. This structure allows for incorporating active learning with a small group of students who have difficulty staying on task with activities in a large class setting. If they are working in a small group of students with a teacher right there to guide them, they are more likely to experience success.

Conclusion

Some of these strategies are staples that you will use every day in every class. However, some of the strategies are useful for certain groups of students that can embrace less structure. Set two goals for yourself. First, just try active learning and incorporate some of the strategies described in this book. You may be surprised at how well your students do. If, however, you are disappointed in their behavior during the activity, then consider how you can add more structure and try again the next time. I have seen middle grades students from all walks of life and all types of backgrounds engage in active learning. So, please do not give up. The second goal to set is to work towards having students manage their behavior through intrinsic motivation rather than extrinsic motivation. Try to remove some of the structure that you have been providing as the year progresses. Guide students toward more independence and encourage them to take more ownership and responsibility for their learning and their behavior.

Chapter 13

Overcoming the Pressure
from Outside the Classroom

If at first you don't succeed, you're probably just like
the teacher in the next classroom. ~Mary Shanley

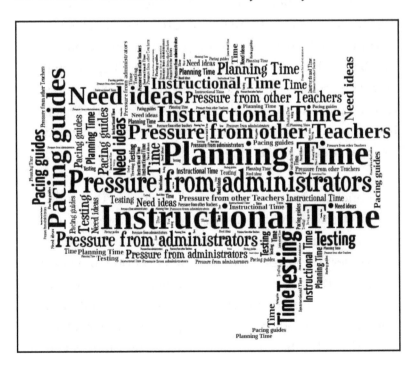

Anyone who has spent five minutes in a middle grades classroom knows that teachers are under immense pressure and stress. It is not a job for the faint of heart. The job is incredibly difficult and complex. Trying to meet the needs of 100 or more young adolescents a day while juggling all of the demands placed on teachers takes incredible skill and almost superhuman powers. And now this book is encouraging you to push even harder and incorporate more active learning than you have before. Will it ever stop?

This chapter deals with the very real issues that make it difficult for teachers to implement active learning. Barriers surround teachers… pressure to increase test scores, rigid district pacing guides, not enough planning time, not enough instructional time, and pressure from other educators to conform to a traditional style of teaching. However, it is possible to overcome those barriers, to incorporate active learning into instruction and prepare students for the standardized test at the same time, and this chapter explains how. The chapter will also share research about teacher self-efficacy and teacher agency. The overall goal of this chapter is to empower you as a teacher to believe that you can have some say in how you teach.

It is important to have the voices of teachers in this book. In this chapter I will be sharing data from a research study regarding nine teachers who incorporate active learning, the barriers they experience, and how they overcome these barriers (Edwards, 2015). I will also share ideas from personal experience in teaching in my own classroom as well as co-teaching with another teacher this past year as part of a research study. I have noted with interest over the years that when I talk about anything related to active learning as an approach to instruction, I am often met with two common reactions. The first reaction is typically a person who smiles and nods his head approvingly and with a hint of excitement says something to the effect of, "tell me more", or "have you got any new ideas that I haven't tried yet?" Those teachers are already sold and are just looking for more ideas. But a distinct second group of teachers have a reaction of a smile and a nod—accompanied by an eye roll. They quickly say that although they have nothing against active learning and in general, it sounds good, it is just not possible in their classroom, with their students, or with the administrative mandates with which they must comply. Interestingly, several times I observed two teachers who taught in the same school and even taught the same students, and one was a strong proponent of active learning and the other said it could not be done. As a result of this observation, I began a research study to try to understand two things. First, I wanted to understand the barriers that teachers face in implementing active learning in their classrooms. Second, I wanted to observe teachers who are able to implement active learning and learn how they were able to overcome those barriers to implement active learning instructional methods in their classrooms.

The teachers who participated in the study were in a variety of schools and worked with a variety of demographics. They worked in urban, rural, and suburban schools that had anywhere from 10% to 99% of their students on free and reduced lunch. Many of these teachers worked in very challenging situations with all types of students who had all types of needs. All of these teachers were under state and district mandates that required conformity to curriculum pacing guides and testing benchmark schedules. Administrators used a very intense teacher evaluation system as they observed these teachers. The system used, among other things, student test scores as data to evaluate the effectiveness of the teachers. This chapter discusses the barriers that these teachers, all of whom regularly implemented active learning instructional approaches, had to overcome.

Real vs. Perceived Barriers

The first question to ask yourself is, are they real barriers or are they perceived barriers? I suspect most teachers are under fewer constraints than they think. Recently, a new teacher mentioned she was struggling with fairly grading her students' writing. She asked the lead teacher on her team for advice and the lead teacher told her, "We don't grade writing." Because she spoke it so emphatically and with such authority, the new teacher figured there must be some school or district policy against grading writing. So, the new teacher started figuring out how to motivate her students to be good writers without grading them. I have a hunch...and I certainly do not know this for a fact...but I have a hunch that there is not a policy against grading writing. I contend that this new teacher could grade her students' writing if she thinks it is the best way to provide feedback. I think that sometimes rules from the bureaucrats above us really don't exist. Teachers have more power to make decisions about what happens in their classrooms than they realize.

If you think there is a policy against using active learning, first, make sure there is a policy prohibiting it. Ask more than one teacher. Better yet, ask an administrator. After administrators have told me in conversations that they are promoting active learning, a teacher in their school has told me that active learning is discouraged in the school. I attribute the disconnect to perception. Sometimes administrators promote, through professional development or some other method, an idea or strategy that they believe will raise test scores. But promoting an idea does not necessarily mean that the administrator believes that is the only effective strategy. For example, a principal's purchase of a set of test-prep workbooks for your subject and grade level does not necessarily mean she wants you to use those workbooks exclusively. Often, mandates of specific programs or instructional methods can be worked into your instruction alongside active learning strategies.

In their book, *Deliberate Optimism: Reclaiming the Joy in Education*, Debbie Silver, Jack Berckemeyer, and Judith Baenen offer these suggestions when faced with obstacles:

1. Before acting or reacting, gather as much information from as many varied sources as possible.

2. Determine what is beyond your control and strategize how to minimize its impact on your life.

3. Establish what you can control and seek tools and strategies to help you maximize your power.

4. Actively do something positive toward your goal.

5. Take ownership of your plan and acknowledge responsibility for your choices. (Silver, Berckemeyer, & Baenen, 2015, p. 7)

This advice works for dealing with the wide range of obstacles teachers face, but is particularly helpful when it comes to implementing active learning. Often what you see as a roadblock turns out to either not be one when you gather more information or is something that can be worked around when you take action on what you can control.

Not Enough Planning Time

The Problem

One of the most common complaints teachers have about implementing active learning in their classrooms is the amount of planning time it takes. It takes more time than planning passive learning when teachers have to find appropriate activities that align with learning objectives, pull together the necessary materials, and think through the logistics of how to implement the activity in a class of 30 students. It is simply quicker to download the worksheet that comes with the textbook.

The teachers in the research study acknowledged the extra time it took to plan active learning instructional methods. They made these comments about the impact of time on planning active learning lessons.

Nick: "If I go home and have a ton of papers to grade, I just don't have the time to plan a great lesson. That can be one of the barriers."

Karina: "Really just the time finding them to me is the greatest thing. You have to *want* to sit there and look for other ways to teach."

Tiffany: "The time it takes to get it done. More so planning it and preparing it. But once I have it I have it."

Pam: "Always time, especially with a new curriculum. Trying to invent. I think we spent so much time this summer just trying to envision what our lesson planning and instruction needed to be."

Possible Solutions

- Be a pack rat. The first solution to this issue comes from Tiffany's idea. As she stated, "…once I have it, I have it." Save everything and reuse it. Many active learning strategies can be used with different content standards. It is possible to recycle something from the first unit and use it again in a later unit in the school year. If you already have the materials on hand, and you have worked through the logistics of implementation, it will take less time to prepare the second time you use the strategy. Additionally, the students will be familiar with the strategy, so there is less class time taken for explaining how the activity will work.

- Organization. Establish files by standard. Once you have those files, download and save ideas, so they are quickly retrievable when it's time to teach that standard. While looking for an idea for one topic, you may find great ideas for three other topics. With a good organizational system, you can readily file those ideas for later use.

- Divide and conquer. "Two heads are better than one" is a good saying. If you can find a colleague who teaches your subject, collaborate to decrease the amount of planning time required. Divide topics or objectives so each person can spend time finding a good activity for different objectives. After you both have ideas for the strategies, divide the labor of planning those activities and gathering the necessary materials. If such a colleague does not teach in your current school, then try to meet teachers who teach your grade and subject at another school.

Not Enough Instructional Time

The Problem

Another problem that teachers express when they implement active learning into their classrooms is the amount of instructional time it takes to do activities. Teachers do not always think that active learning is the most efficient method in terms of instructional time. Here are some comments from the teachers in the research study:

Erin: "You can't do as much as you used to… there are certain—we have curriculum maps—there are certain nine weeks where it's a little tighter, like the last one, it's tight to get everything in."

Clarisa: "Time is one, because you've got so much to teach that you feel like you've got to take the time to find out who the kids are. But I don't always have time necessarily because I've got to do x, y, z to get them ready for the benchmark."

Aaron: "It's always the pressure that we are under now. It's not that educators are not trying to make work engaging, but we have so much to get through, and not me per se, but I know what my fellow teachers are going through because they have to get this done in a certain time. Yes, we could do this assignment, the fun assignment, but we don't have time for it."

Possible Solutions

- Really learning something is worth 10 worksheets. Please consider that completing worksheets does not necessarily result in real learning. Sometimes middle grades students are simply writing answers to a worksheet to "look busy", and they are not really learning the material in front of them. If you are able to find an effective strategy that engages students in the content, the probability is higher that they will actually learn the content. Worksheet completion does not automatically equal learning.

- Kill two birds with one stone. A quality active learning project can incorporate more than one standard. By integrating more than one concept into a significant active learning approach, you can actually use the same amount of class time that you would have used teaching the two concepts separately.

We Have to Get Them Ready for the Test

The Problem

The most common reason teachers give for not incorporating active learning in their classrooms is standardized testing. Anecdotally, many teachers report that active learning cannot be implemented in the current climate of standardized testing and accountability (Vaughn, 2013; Wood, 2004). McEwin and Greene (2010) report in their survey of randomly selected middle schools that 81% of respondents reported regularly using direct instruction, while 64% of respondents reported regularly using cooperative learning, and only 42% of respondents regularly used inquiry teaching. They found that "schools still tend to rely more heavily on teacher-centered direct instruction" (p. 55). Musoleno and White (2010) also conclude that developmentally appropriate instructional practices that are aligned with middle school philosophy have decreased since the No Child Left Behind Act increased the pressure of standardized testing on schools and teachers.

Possible Solutions

- The reality is that if you teach something well, and students really learn it with deep understanding, it does not matter what format the assessment is. If you were given a test on your name and the name of all your family members, you would have no problem passing that test, regardless of whether you were asked a constructed-response question or a multiple-choice question, because you have lived and experienced your family. The same can hold true for academic content. If your students have experienced the content in an active way, they will be more likely to really know that content and to demonstrate their understanding in whatever form they are assessed, including multiple-choice.

- Some teachers argue that students need to practice the multiple-choice format if that is the way they will be assessed. Rest assured that by the time students in the United States reach middle school, they have been sufficiently exposed to the multiple-choice format and understand how it works. Really. They have had plenty of practice. Students have had less practice at applying their knowledge through authentic assessments...you can be the teacher that gives them those opportunities.

- Here's a secret... they are just writing letters down. This may surprise you if you are convinced that every student pours over every test-prep question and diligently thinks through the alternatives. Many students are just randomly writing the letters A, B, C, and D so that they can "look busy." Having students write what they know or demonstrate what they know in an active format will give you more accurate information about their true conceptual understanding.

- At least turn it into a game. If you are compelled to use test-prep questions, at least make a game of it. Students will be more motivated to work at finding the correct answer if points for their team are at stake.

Pressure from Other Teachers

The Problem

Anecdotally some teachers will admit that they want to implement active learning but feel pressure from other teachers to do traditional, teacher-directed instruction. One difficulty teachers have is that they co-plan with other teachers of the same subject that teach the same grade level. If you are the only teacher in the group who has an active learning philosophy and the other teachers are advocates of passive learning, there is pressure to conform. New teachers on a team of veteran teachers will find this especially challenging.

As I am writing this book I am doing a research study in which I co-teach with a beginning teacher who believes strongly in active learning. Here are some of her comments:

Karen: "In the one school where I was able to implement active learning, you had to be in the hallway during every class change. One teacher would walk by and poke fun at me: 'Oh, it must be nice to play games every day. What game are you playing today?' Every day that I had any kind of active learning he would have something to say. I wish I could find somebody who was willing to do it with me."

Although Karen wants to teach in innovative ways, she finds herself adapting to the veteran teachers around her.

Karen: "I'm like a chameleon. I become like whoever I am around. I hope this doesn't change me for the worse…I feel myself getting sucked into that mindset and way of teaching."

This powerful force pulls on a lot of new teachers making them become like the veteran teachers that surround them. That force includes attitude, dispositions towards students, approach to the content, thoughts about instruction, and work ethic.

Another issue can be the age-old social issue of just being different as seen in Tammi, a third year teacher participating in a research study by Margaret Vaughn (2013). Tammi lamented, "I'm the only one it seems that's teaching this way [creatively and student-centered] and it's like putting a big target on my back. People say, okay, why is her classroom not like everyone else's" (Vaughn, 2013, p. 126)? Tammi, like many other teachers, wanted to teach in a student-centered manner that involved more active learning, rather than passive learning, but she didn't want to be the only one teaching in that manner. It is difficult to be the only teacher doing anything. There are subtle pressures from students, from parents, and from other teachers that make it more desirable to be like everyone else. It is ironic how, in this way, middle school teachers are not much different than middle school students. We want to be part of the norm rather than standing out by being too different.

Possible Solutions

- When planning with teachers who have a traditional mindset or a teaching philosophy other than yours, come in to the meeting with an active learning strategy already planned thoroughly. Understandably, many teachers find it comfortable to pull out the worksheet they used last year. The expectations for teachers are so many and so high that there simply is not enough time to do it all. When you come in with a new idea, they may hear: "I have this great fancy idea that is going to take a lot of work to put together and the kids may all go nuts while doing it. So, don't you want to stay up tonight putting this new activity together even though you already have one you like?" If you are willing to do the legwork and come in with the strategy already planned out, they may be more open to it. Perhaps over time you can talk your team members into an active learning strategy here and there if you do not overwhelm them with a lot of extra work.

- Another possibility when planning with veteran teachers who have an arsenal of worksheets for every topic is to take the group plan and spice it up. In some schools, teams are required to plan together and follow the same lesson plan. This can be problematic if everyone else on your team disagrees with the idea of active learning. Often, you can easily adapt a traditional lesson plan by adding some active learning strategies to it. So, take their basic lesson plan and change the structure. For example, if a PowerPoint is listed, include some interactive lecture

strategies from Chapter 5. If a worksheet is listed, include
a small group strategy from Chapter 3 or a game from
Chapter 6.

- Get thicker skin when other teachers criticize you. Who
cares if they mock you? The proof is in the pudding…or
the test scores. If you are convinced that active learning
is important for middle grades students and you do
it well, they will learn. At the end of the day, if your
students are learning, that is what is truly important,
not what other teachers think of you. Incorporate active
learning strategies to the extent that you are allowed by
administration, even if others are not.

- Find a support system, even if it is with teachers who do
not teach at your school, or even in your school system.
At professional conferences look for teachers who also
support active learning. You will meet a lot of eager and
motivated teachers at professional conferences sponsored
by organizations such as the Association for Middle
Level Education (AMLE). Another place to find good
colleagues with whom to collaborate is online. While
having colleagues committed to active learning at your
school is ideal, online colleagues that can support you
can be helpful as well on those days when you need a little
encouragement or an idea of how to make something
work better.

Pressure from Administrators

The Problem

Many teachers who desire to do more student-centered
instruction with an emphasis on active learning lament that

directives from administrators prevent them from doing so. Many administrators, whether they are building principals or district administrators, require teachers to follow rigid policies with regard to instruction. The policies can relate to structures for lessons, teacher-directed curriculum materials, and test-prep practices. In today's standardized testing culture, teachers are often required to do more and more assessment and are allowed less freedom in terms of selecting approaches to instruction (Musoleno & White, 2010; Vaughn, 2013).

Possible Solutions

- Do a little PR. Both parents and administrators will give you the benefit of the doubt if you communicate what you are doing and how it helps your students.

- Use research to back up your claims. See the research appendix in the back of this book for a sample of research studies that support the use of active learning with young adolescents.

- Convince your principal with data. Use pre- and post-assessments on a given standard. Show him that your students are learning. Be sure to include different levels of questions. Show that your students can answer the multiple-choice questions like they will see on the standardized test, but also include some higher-level constructed-response questions to demonstrate that active learning will actually take students to a deeper level.

- See it from the perspective of your principal. In general, the two biggest concerns of the typical principal are discipline and test scores. If you can convince her that you have these under control, she will give you more autonomy to make decisions about your instruction. By the way, students behave better if they are not bored.

- When required to do teacher-proof materials or test-prep materials, do them, but that does not have to be all that you do. You can incorporate them through a game, or supplement the test-prep materials with other more engaging activities. You can do good teaching most of the period and do a little test-prep on the side so that you can stay in line with policies or directives from administrators.

Need More Ideas

The Problem

One struggle that most of the teachers in the active learning research study (Edwards, 2015) mentioned was that they just "need more ideas" and the time to find those ideas.

> Keisha: "You just run out of ideas... when you run out of things to do and you say, 'I am overusing groups', 'I'm overusing working with a peer', 'I'm overusing the computers', because they become overreliant on it."

Possible Solutions

- Observe other teachers. Even if they teach a different subject, you can often take an active learning strategy and adapt it to fit your content. You will learn a tremendous amount from just being in different classrooms and talking with different teachers.

Keisha:	"Seeing what the lower level teachers do actually has helped. We do vertical alignment, and I had an opportunity to see what they were doing. They had those kids on the floor with the manipulatives and doing other things like that. The kids were engaged, and I thought, 'If they can do that in the lower grades, definitely my fifth graders can do that.' So, I try them, they work, and the kids really enjoyed it. We are going to do this from now on. And I've been sticking with it."
Tiffany:	"It helps me to see you do a strategy and then I feel confident doing the same strategy in my other classes. I have to see it work first."

- Consider all possible resources. In addition to asking other teachers, you can ask professionals outside of teaching. Business and industry partners can be valuable for sharing expertise and creating active learning opportunities for students. Some of the best classes where you will see real student engagement are days when a guest speaker from outside comes into the school. They can bring relevance and authentic learning to your content. The Internet also has a wealth of ideas that can be found on teacher blogs, Pinterest, and websites devoted to inquiry learning or project-based learning.

Crystal:	"I haven't really found the time to get new ideas, but I am just making the time. If I didn't know where to look for resources, I would email somebody else, and for the most part, people are friendly and helpful. For example, I emailed a professor at Skidway Institute to get him to come up and talk about plate tectonics and how often Georgia has earthquakes...He couldn't come during our unit, but he helped by sending me some resources, and I think that's neat. So, everybody I have made contact with has been able to help me to get new ideas for my lessons."

Requires More Effort

The Problem

Several teachers admitted that truly implementing active learning requires more effort on the part of the teacher than teaching passive learning strategies. They suggested the possibility that some teachers may not be willing to devote the necessary time and effort. Katherine claimed, "I really think it's about a teacher's comfort level... it's hard to have a lot of different activities. It's easier just to throw out a worksheet or a PowerPoint that's created." And Crystal acknowledged that the more challenging active learning approach requires the teacher to make a shift.

Crystal: "Just getting out of your comfort zone [is new]. Letting go [is new]. We are so used to direct instruction, whole class in rows, and then when we are really determined to shake it up, we put two desks together. So, I'm really doing something."

Crystal: "For the most part, what we have to do is dull, and the dull version is extremely easy on us. This [active learning] takes your willingness to go a little bit further. You may do the lesson plan and then you probably want to tweak it again... this didn't really work out... Sometimes we actually have to take it home and have our burst of inspiration or to make sure that we're engaging them with some good quality, active learning."

Possible Solutions

- The obvious suggestion here is to just roll up your sleeves and put the effort into it. Not intending to insult middle grades teachers who are already overworked and underpaid, I will not insult you by suggesting it can be done with no or minimal effort.

- Divide and conquer. Two heads are better than one, and three heads are even better than two. If you can find someone willing to share the load with you, you can minimize the effort either one of you has to carry. Take turns developing activities and gathering materials.

- Do not reinvent the wheel. There are thousands of great ideas online.

- Be a pack rat. Collect ideas from everywhere, even if you think you do not need them. Have an organization system where you can file ideas for potential use in the future. Over the years, I have adapted many things originally intended for a different purpose.

Powerful Influence of Educational Tradition

The Problem

I currently teach both undergraduate and graduate pre-service teachers. One night in class, I was talking about young adolescent physical development and related it to the need to incorporate movement into the classroom. I shared one simple active learning strategy that can be used in different content areas. I was surprised by one of the student's questions. Micah said that he really liked all of the ideas that I shared in class and wanted to teach in that way, but he was concerned. He said, "Will we get in trouble if we do this? I mean, I don't see other teachers doing things like this. Will we get in trouble if we have the students doing all of these activities?" This question actually made me a little sad that the culture of our schools has gotten so fixed that the idea of actively engaging students in learning content seems abnormal and risky.

Educational tradition is a powerful force. The idea of the teacher standing up and sharing his or her wisdom with students who quietly listen has been around for centuries.

Most of us experienced traditional teacher-directed instruction when we were in school, and so we naturally replicate that in our own teaching. Finally, to be quite honest, doing something different requires risk and can create some discomfort and anxiety (Bonwell & Eison, 1991).

Possible Solutions

- Take a risk and just try it. Try incorporating a project or a few active learning strategies into the next unit that you teach and watch how the students respond. You will be pleasantly surprised at how much more involved with the content your students will be.

Tiffany: "I was out at Greenwood Middle one semester. The kids were always getting in trouble, and the teacher was always making them write the school pledge. In the lesson that I taught, students created those boxes with different information on the sides, and I saw how into it those kids were. That's what convinced me to do more active learning."

Research on Overcoming Barriers

This section includes the thoughts of real middle school teachers who believe in active learning. They deal with all of the challenges listed above, yet remain committed to active learning. Through observation and interview data, there were three common characteristics of these teachers that directly supported their ability to overcome the barriers and to incorporate active learning in their instruction. The teachers were tenacious, student-focused, and experimental (Edwards, 2015).

Tenacious

When asked how they were able to get their students engaged in active learning despite all of the barriers, the teachers used phrases such as "you just do it" and "you have to be very determined." These teachers demonstrated a tenacious determination to teach the way they believed was best for their students. Here are examples of their tenacity:

Nick: "It's a challenge to do all these things, but I am going to do what I have to do to make sure my kids know everything."

Erin: "You know, we just make it work, and find time somewhere to do it."

Clarisa: "You just do it, you just figure it out."

Keisha: "I'm going to give you all of me but I expect you to give all of you, too. It is possible. It's about your willingness to do it. This is what's necessary. It's the non-negotiable as far as education."

Katherine: "That's just how it is. So, you've got to figure out a way to work it out. You make it happen."

Pam: "I think it's tenacity, you can't just give it up... I think it's a commitment that you just have to make. If you throw your hands up and say, "It can't be done," then you've kind of made your mind up that it can't be done. Sometimes it's just persistence."

Erin: "I guess cause I'm just willing to keep trying."

Karina: "I think it's just that I try to find ways to do it. I think you also have to have the incentive or desire to go out and put this extra time and effort into it. That's what you go to work for. You don't do it half way. I think it's that. That is what has been inserted in me my whole life. You do the best you can, otherwise what's the point?"

Crystal: "I guess cause I'm just willing to keep trying."

Student-Focused

When interviewing the teachers, they rarely spoke about themselves and answered most of the questions by talking about their students. They were very student-focused and always spoke about making instructional decisions in terms of the impact on the students. Examining how their students responded to their instruction increased their commitment to active learning. The relationships the teachers had with their students were an important part of the learning that takes place in the classroom. Here are some examples of the teachers' comments:

Nick: "It's important to make sure your kids are actually getting it."

Keisha: "You start to care a whole lot... and the look of frustration on a kid's face is painful to me. I don't want them to be frustrated with something I taught."

Erin: "When it comes down to the classroom, when you shut the door and it's you and the kids, you've got to do something that keeps them going and makes them want to learn."

Aaron: "When I think of my kids, I think that when they come into my room, they're excited to be here most of the time. The same kids that you probably just saw in another classroom, you would see them disengaged... You know you have to have something they enjoy... They're engaged, and I know, and I see that in them."

Clarisa: "It's really important to make sure that they learn it differently and that we teach it differently for them. But if you don't know your kids, then you can't do that."

Keisha: "Because the kids said, "I love going to
            your class". "I did your homework last
            night". When they tell you things like that,
            it kind of makes you want to serve them.
            That's what I'm here for—to serve them."

Katherine: It's vital in learning. We have to value
            the kids that we have because number
            one, that's providing us a job, but it's our
            job to be prepared to teach them, to keep
            them engaged. To provide them the best
            education that we can provide for them,
            and we have to do different types
            of teaching."

Keisha: "I guess just seeing when they sit there and
            their eyes glaze over, I can't stand that. So,
            how can I get this information to you? So,
            I feel like they would be wasting their time,
            if I don't do this."

Crystal: "So, I try to make it where it's real life for
            them, even the ones that don't like science,
            I'm trying to pique their interest enough,
            where it's: "I thought social studies was
            my best subject but I really like science."
            So, but it's always got to be hands-on and
            active for them."

Keisha	I want to be fun. School should not be boring. So many schools should not be boring. That's what's going to keep the kids. Having fun at school keeps our kids. Because if you are not having fun, they are not going to be here trying to learn anything from you. So I want them to have fun."
Aaron:	"Having the kids engaged, this is very important as well because if kids are not engaged, they are not going to respond. They are not going to learn because they don't care about the information. Having an engaged curriculum… if kids are bored, they're not going to learn."

Experimental

A third quality that all of the teachers possessed was a willingness to experiment, to take risks, to try new things, and to make adjustments to their instruction if it was not working for their students. They got ideas from a variety of sources including other colleagues, the Internet, professional development, as well as their own creativity. Here are some of their thoughts:

Pam: "I can't tell you how many times we start something, even eighth grade this year, we're just revamping our curriculum. We start it and we go, and nope that didn't work. We have to change it midstream. So, I think being prepared is something you almost do—You prepare, you hope for the best. But during a class, you might have to go, nope that's not working, so let's just back up and try it this way…and rather than pushing them to the frustration level, sometimes you have to back up [and try something else]."

Clarisa: "I guess that I am willing to do it; a lot of teachers are not willing to try something different to think outside of the box. I am willing to try anything once as long as it's not going to hurt anybody. I'm willing to try it, and if it doesn't work, we will go back and revamp, redo it the next day, and figure it out."

Nick: "Really just watching other teachers has helped me a lot. I have my own way of teaching, but it also helps feeding off others' ideas. The Internet helps to find stuff, asking other teachers, talking to other teachers to see what they are doing."

Karina: "We do teacher observations or peer observations... "Ooo, I like how she did that..." "I want to try that..." I have actually gone over to the high school since we are life science and they do biology to see how they do things and then bring stuff back here. So, I hate to say it, but it's just a lot of 'I like that'... 'I'd like to try that'... just bring it in and go with it."

Erin: "I guess always looking for new ideas... and I have some things I do every year that I know work really well...'this really teaches this concept, I'm going to keep it.' You know, kids have changed so much that things we used to do with them just aren't as motivating anymore because they have so many electronics and things of that nature. So, [I use] things that work, and labs I know are great and going to get a great response out of the kids. It's always kind of been my nature [to go out and figure things out]. If something fails, then try something new the next time."

Clarisa:	"Are there days when I say 'This isn't working we have to go with plan B'—sure, but for the most part, we will tweak, usually after first period. It's the same concept but it will look completely different during sixth period. One, because the kids are different, and two, because I have worked the kinks out during the day. I know how to work it out to be more efficient for them in terms of their learning time. You don't ever stop tweaking and fixing and moving along."
Katherine:	"I have a big binder of my unit plan, and every time I do something, I put it in there. If I find a new activity, I shove it in there. That way every year, when I'm looking at the unit, I have lots of things to do and I write notes. What worked… what didn't work. Why this one particular group activity did not work and how I could have made it better. Every day… for the most part… Every day or every other day, we are doing something new."
Crystal:	"And there's only so many bag of tricks… items in a bag of tricks but then you have to put your own spin on them. So, I've been able to take these little snippits of everywhere I've gone and put them in bag and been able to use them."

Aaron: "I have gotten ideas from going to graduate school and learning new strategies, and thinking okay, I think I can pick this up, and I think I will try it in my classroom."

Clarisa: "I do spend a good bit of time doing peer observations; and when somebody says, 'Such and such is doing something great in their room,' I go find out what they are doing. It might be a math class, but I can take that concept of the teaching philosophy and incorporate it—'oh, I can use that in social studies when we get to something else.' I beg and borrow and don't wanna' say *steal*, but here, we steal and we reinvent for ourselves. There is a lot of stuff on the Internet that is great stuff, and I can take bits and pieces, and tweak it to work for my class. That saved me from having to reinvent the wheel. I can take and piece it together with my own little crazy flair on it. That leaves me more time to take care of other stuff. So, I'm not reinventing the wheel but I'm taking the extra time to do that."

Teacher Vision, Teacher Agency, and Teacher Self-Efficacy

"What is a classroom? A place for students and teachers. Students struggle, succeed, fail, give up, try again. Teachers struggle, succeed, fail, give up, try again." ~Esther Wright

• • • • • • • • • • •

A Tale of Two Teachers

I would like to describe two teachers that I know, Bill and Nicole. Both learned the same active learning principles in their teacher education courses. Both were exposed to principles and theories that support the notion of active learning and learned strategies for implementing active learning in real middle school classrooms. Both had some experience incorporating active learning in their field experience classrooms while in college. Both Bill and Nicole expressed great enthusiasm for the notion of active learning and stated that they were definitely planning for their own future classrooms to have a heavy dose of active learning on a daily basis. They were sold.

The two teachers ended up in different schools in the same school district, which of course, have different contexts. Bill took a position teaching sixth grade math in a rural middle school. Required to plan with two veteran math teachers, he was told to follow their lead and match their lesson plans. Nicole took a position in an urban middle school teaching seventh grade math. Required to plan with two other math teachers, she was told to follow the lead of the veteran teachers and match their lesson plans. So, the two had very similar teacher preparation experiences, both were first year teachers, both began their careers with strong beliefs that active learning is important for middle grades students, and both were in challenging teaching situations.

Not surprisingly, they both found their first year of teaching overwhelming. They struggled to keep up with the workload, implement all of the administrative mandates, and deal with the wide variety of needs their students had. Neither of the teachers sailed through the year with feet propped up sipping lemonade. Both worked harder than ever before in their lives.

Fast-forward a year. If you were to walk into the two classrooms today, you would assume that the two teachers had very different teaching philosophies. You would assume that Bill has a firm belief in behaviorism and a teacher-directed instructional philosophy. You would assume that Nicole has a belief in constructivism and an active learning philosophy. Both teachers would readily admit they have a lot to learn and are still growing in their teaching practice. They would talk humbly about the challenges they experienced, but somehow Nicole was able to enact her belief system and regularly incorporate active learning into her instruction. Why is that?

● ● ● ● ● ● ● ● ● ●

Teacher's Vision

Some teachers possess a clear vision of basing their teaching on how they think students learn best. Duffy (2002) characterizes a teacher's vision as "a personal stance on teaching that rises from deep within the inner teacher and fuels independent thinking" (p. 334). He also suggests that a teacher's vision incorporates his or her "passions, hopes, cares, and dreams" (p. 334). It is more than just a method learned in a college course; it is based on a deeply held personal commitment and moral conviction about how students learn. Hammerness (2001) refers to a set of images of ideal classroom practice to which teachers strive. In other words, a teacher who has a vision that includes active learning pictures himself or herself in the classroom with students engaged in active learning. That vision must rise out of a deeply held personal belief system that active learning is important and that it works for young adolescents.

Research suggests that teachers who possess a clear vision are more likely to teach according to their convictions and to assume control over instructional decision making in spite of district pressures to standardize instruction and to emphasize test preparation (Duffy, 2002; Duffy & Hoffman, 1999). These teachers have the fortitude to enact their vision despite the constraints imposed on them from administrators and the pressures they may feel to use "teacher proof" curricula and test-prep materials. They know what they believe about what is best for their students, and they possess the confidence to enact instruction in line with their visions. They are more likely to have the strength to adapt their instruction to the needs of their students and to teach responsively (Vaughn & Faircloth, 2011). Teachers with vision are able to invent and modify, rather than emulate (Duffy, 2002). Shulman and Shulman (2004) suggest that teachers with vision are more likely to reflect on their practice, evaluate the effectiveness of their instruction, and to imagine possibilities based on what their students need.

Teacher Self-Efficacy

If you have a vision for a classroom where students are regularly engaged in active learning, if that is what you truly want to happen, then the next step is to believe that it can happen. You need to believe that you are capable of figuring out how to get around any barriers that you encounter so that you can successfully lead that classroom. Scholars refer to that belief system as teacher self-efficacy. Bandura (1997) defined self-efficacy as, "beliefs in one's capabilities to organize and execute the courses of action required to produce given attainments" (p.3). Tschannen-Moran and Hoy (2001) defined teacher efficacy as a teacher's "judgment of his or her capabilities to bring about desired outcomes of student engagement and learning, even among those students who may be difficult or unmotivated" (p. 783). Basically, your self-efficacy as a teacher is how much you feel you have the power to implement the vision you have in your mind. A teacher with low self-efficacy believes he is at the mercy of administrative mandates, the types of students assigned to him, the quality of parenting of those students, or the colleagues with whom he works. A teacher with high self-efficacy believes she can make her vision happen in her classroom in spite of all of the contextual factors. That teacher believes she has an impact on how her students learn.

Self-efficacy beliefs are a good predictor of how teachers behave. What we believe influences where we put our effort and how much effort we put forth. We will put our efforts where we believe they will be worthwhile (Bandura, 1986). Since teachers have limited time and are pulled in many directions with multiple responsibilities, it is logical for them to put forth time and effort in things they believe they have control of. Self-efficacy is related to past successes and is linked to reflecting on those successes when faced with current challenges. Castle (2006) claims that when teachers reflect on their practice, it bolsters their autonomy and motivates them to make decisions about future purposeful actions that will achieve success. Students of teachers who have a strong sense of self-efficacy benefit from those teachers' tendency to take more instructional risks, to experiment with different instructional methods and to continually seek to improve their instruction (Allinder, 1994; Guskey, 1988; Stein & Wang, 1988). Students of teachers with high self-efficacy also have higher levels of performance (Moore & Esselman, 1992; Anderson, Greene, & Loewen, 1988; Ross, 1992).

It is important for you to put your focus on two things over which you have control: your choices and your effort (Bandura, 1986). It is true that there are mandates from administration that teachers are obliged to follow. But not everything is mandated. "It is both disconcerting and empowering to realize that most of our present situations are shaped by the choices we made and the amount of deliberate effort we were willing to put forth" (Silver, Berckemeyer, & Baenen, 2015, p.31). Focus your effort on those things within your control and make choices that allow you to move closer to the active learning classroom that you hope for.

Teacher Agency

But obviously, just believing that active learning will improve your student's achievement is not enough if you do not enact that type of instruction in your classroom. Believing that you can do it and that your students will benefit is the beginning, but belief must translate into action. This action is referred to by scholars as teacher agency. Oakeshott and Fuller (2001) refer to agency as the "starting place of doing" (p. 35). Teacher agency describes teachers who, based on their visions and beliefs, work to teach according to their beliefs, even in the midst of restrictive policies and other challenges (Vaughn & Faircloth, 2011). In short, teacher agency is a teacher's ability to act on his or her vision, beliefs, and convictions. Greene (1978) proposes that this may also "carry with it a conviction of moral responsibility" (p. 248). Danielewicz (2001) argued that teachers must have the will "to act, to make decisions, and to participate" (p. 163). Teacher agency can be seen in a teacher who initiates intentional action in order to enact a specific purpose in a thoughtful manner and with autonomy (Bandura, 2001; Epstein, 2007).

Teachers with agency are not followers, they are independent thinkers. They evaluate what they learn from a variety of sources and work around restrictive directives to achieve their vision. They make decisions that are consistent with their convictions and their personal beliefs about what is best for their students (Duffy, 2002). Scholars have identified other characteristics of these teachers. They have a sense of perceived control (Zimmerman, 1995), a sense of personal empowerment (Danielewicz, 2001), they are persistent (Bandura, 2001, Edwards, 2015), they have initiative (Arendt, 1958; Bandura, 2001), and they are reflective (Dewey, 1933; Schon, 1987; Zeichner & Liston, 1996). These teachers are able to implement their vision in the face of challenges and are able to negotiate the obstacles that get in the way in order to achieve their goals (Vaughn, 2013).

Duckworth, Quinn, and Seligman (2009) completed an interesting research study that helps explain why some teachers are able to effectively implement instructional strategies such as active learning in the face of challenges. They studied 390 novice teachers who had similar teacher preparation and were all placed in under-resourced public schools. The study found that three qualities were better predictors of teacher effectiveness than traditional qualities such as education and teacher preparation. The teachers who exhibited higher levels of grit, life satisfaction, and optimistic explanatory style saw their students make higher academic gains.

- *Grit*—is defined as "perseverance and passion for long-term goals. Gritty individuals tend to work harder than equally able peers, and they remain committed to their chosen pursuits longer" (p. 541).

- *Life satisfaction*—is the idea of contentment with your current life situation. People with high life satisfaction experience more frequent positive moods. This could be helpful in the classroom because students are more likely to be drawn to teachers who are happy.

- *Optimistic explanatory style*—is the idea that a person can influence adverse events through their own actions rather than exhibiting a state of learned helplessness.

• • • • • • • • • • •

Back to Bill and Nicole. The theories on teacher visioning, teacher self-efficacy, and teacher agency can be seen in Bill and Nicole's stories. Bill did have a vision for his classroom, but he had a low self-efficacy. He felt that he had to exactly follow the administrative mandate to plan with other teachers and thought that meant his lessons had to look exactly like theirs. He succumbed to the pressure of the veteran teachers he was assigned to work with and felt powerless to do anything other than follow the teacher-directed lessons they planned. He felt obligated to follow their lead even though the instructional practices were contrary to what he believed was best for his students. He felt that as a new teacher, he had no choice but to march along in lock-step with the other mathematics teachers.

Nicole, on the other hand, was able to navigate similar restrictive mandates. Nicole not only had a strong vision for her classroom, she had a strong sense of self-efficacy. She believed that as a teacher she has the power to control the instruction in her classroom. She took that belief further and acted on those beliefs with agency. She did plan with the other teachers, but she adapted the agreed-upon plans to incorporate active learning methods. She observed other teachers who incorporated active learning and learned from them. She saw strategies that were effective with other teachers and became convinced that she could do those same strategies with her students and that they would be just as effective with her students. When she tried something that did not work, she would reflect, regroup, adjust and modify, and try again. Nicole had an active learning vision for her classroom, a strong sense of self-efficacy and belief that her students could learn through active learning, and a strong sense of agency that motivated her to enact that vision. You can, too.

• • • • • • • • • • •

You've heard the stories...

Michael Jordan was cut from his high school basketball team.

Abraham Lincoln was defeated in eight elections.

Thomas Edison was told by his teacher that he was too stupid to learn anything.

Lucille Ball was dismissed from drama school because they thought she was too shy.

Albert Einstein was not able to speak until he was four years old.

Oprah Winfrey was demoted from her job as a news anchor because she wasn't fit for television.

Walt Disney was fired from a newspaper for lacking imagination.

Steve Jobs was removed from the company he started.

The Beatles were rejected by a recording studio that said they had no future in show business.

Dr. Seuss had his first book rejected by 27 publishers.

J. K. Rowling was penniless and trying to raise a child on her own while attending school.

Elvis Presley was fired after one performance and told he should go back to driving a truck.

Harrison Ford was told by movie executives that he didn't have what it takes to be a star.

Jerry Seinfeld was booed off the stage at his first performance.

All of these people accomplished really hard things. They are famous because they accomplished their vision. I am sure that like you and me, they had obstacles and barriers in their way. It was not easy to do the things that they did. But they possessed more than a vision; they possessed self-efficacy and agency. They made it happen. Yes, teaching using active learning methodology has inherent challenges. But is it impossible? No. If Michael and Abraham can do their thing, you can, too.

I wish school had us think like this more. I feel like a
Zombie all day. ~Tamika, 7th grade

Research about
Active Learning

Adams, J. (2009). *The impact of kinesthetic activities on eighth grade benchmark scores* (Unpublished master's thesis). Melrose Park, PA: Gratz College.

A research study on kinesthetic activities with eighth graders. Kinesthetic activities in the classroom were found to create student enthusiasm, assist in increasing benchmark scores, and enhance the total academic experience for eighth grade students.

Ambrose, S., Bridges, M., DiPietro, M., Lovett, M., & Norman, M. (2010). *How learning works: Seven research-based principles for smart teaching.* San Francisco: Jossey-Bass.

A summary of research on how students learn.

Bonwell, C., & Eison, J. (1991). *Active learning: Creating excitement in the classroom.* (ASHE-ERIC Higher Education Report No. 1). Washington, DC: The George Washington University, School of Education and Human Development.

A summary of research on active learning and student achievement.

Caine, R., Caine, G., McClintic, C., & Klimek, K. (2009). *12 brain/mind learning principles in action: Developing executive functions of the human brain* (2nd ed.). Thousand Oaks, CA: Corwin.

A summary of research about how the brain learns.

Carbonneau, K. J., Marley, S. C., & Selig, J. P. (2013). A meta-analysis of the efficacy of teaching mathematics with concrete manipulatives. *Journal of Educational Psychology, 105*(2), 380–400. doi: 10.1037/a0031084

A meta-analysis of 55 research studies of students in kindergarten through college. Manipulatives can produce a positive effect on student learning. The use of manipulatives in mathematics has the greatest effect on retention, with small effects on problem solving, transfer, and justification.

Capraro, M., Capraro, R., Carter, T., & Harbaugh, A. (2010). Understanding, questioning, and representing mathematics: What makes a difference in middle school classrooms? *Research in Middle Level Education, 34*(4), 1–18.

A research study in sixth grade classrooms that
found Teaching Quality Measures improved
student performance.

Cornelius-White, J., & Harbaugh, A. (2010). *Learner-centered instruction: Building relationships for student success.*
Thousand Oaks, CA: Sage.

A review of research on learner-centered instruction,
including active learning.

DePew, J., Moss, G., & Swim, T. (2009). Engaging rural-urban
students in creative writing. *scholarlypartnershipsedu, 4*(2).

A narrative analysis of a teacher who uses project-
based learning with high school students in an urban-
rural school as a means of improving test preparation.
The authors saw increases in student understanding,
leadership, knowledge of business, and an identification
of creative talents.

Dias, M., Eick, C. J., & Brantly-Dias, L. (2011). Practicing
what we teach: A self-study in implementing an inquiry-based
curriculum in a middle grades classroom. *Journal for Science
Teacher Education, 22,* 53–78. doi: 10.1007/s10972-010-9222-z

A self-study of a science teacher returning to teach middle
grades students after teaching at the collegiate level. The
use of inquiry pedagogy with a reform-based curriculum
on middle grades students to create a more responsive,
student-driven learning environment is examined.

DiCamillo, L., & Gradwell, J. (2012). Using simulations to teach middle grades U.S. history in an age of accountability. *Research in Middle Level Education, 35*(7), 1–16.

A year-long qualitative study in two eighth grade U.S. History classrooms. The teachers used simulations on a regular basis to teach students in a high-stakes learning environment. The study found active participation or acting as a facilitator during simulations aids in engaging students in the learning process.

DiCecco, V., & Gleason, M. (2002). Using graphic organizers to attain relational knowledge from expository text. *Journal of Learning Disabilities, 35*(4), 306–320.

A study of middle school students with learning disabilities during a social studies unit on how technology affected life in the United States in the 1920s. The study found that graphic organizers enhance both comprehension and memory and, therefore, serve as powerful learning tools for all students.

Feinstein, S. (2009). *Secrets of the teenage brain: Research-based strategies for reaching and teaching today's adolescents* (2nd ed.). Thousand Oaks, CA: Corwin Press.

A review of brain-based research and teaching adolescents.

Finn, K. E., & McInnis, K. J. (2014). Teachers' and students' perceptions of the active science curriculum: Incorporating physical activity into middle school science classrooms. *Physical Educator, 71*(2), 234–253.

A research study with two science teachers and fifth and sixth grade students examining students' and teachers' perceptions regarding incorporating physical activity into a middle school science curriculum. The study found that incorporating physical activity into lessons made learning fun and exciting. It also helped behaviors such as alertness, focus, and concentration.

Fogarty, R. (2009) *Brain-compatible classrooms* (3rd Ed.). Victoria, Australia: Hawker Brownlow.

A summary of brain research that helps teachers understand how to build high-achievement classrooms.

Gehlbach, H., Brown, S. W., Ioannou, A., Boyer, M. A., Hudson, N., Niv-Solomon, A., Maneggia, D., & Janik, L. (2008). Increasing interest in social studies: Social perspective taking and self-efficacy in stimulating simulations. *Contemporary Educational Psychology, 33*(4), 894–914. doi:10.1016/j.cedpsych.2007.11.002

A research study of 305 middle grades students from 19 schools across the United States examining the use of simulations to boost middle school student interest in social studies. The study found increases in student motivation after they experienced a web-based GlobalEd simulation.

Goldsby, D. (2009). *Research summary: Manipulatives in middle grades mathematics.* Retrieved from http://www.amle.org/TabId/270/ArtMID/888/ArticleID/325/Research-Summary-Manipulatives-in-Middle-Grades-Mathematics.aspx

A research summary on the use of manipulatives to teach mathematics in the middle grades.

Hernandez-Ramos, P., & De La Paz, S. (2009). Learning history in middle school by designing multimedia in a project-based learning experience. *Journal of Research on Technology in Education, 42*(2), 151–173.

A study of eighth grade students who created multimedia mini-documentaries while studying 19th century United States History. The study found significant learning gains as well as growth in historical thinking skills.

Hyerle, D., & Alper, L. (2011). Student successes with thinking maps. *School-based research, results, and models for achievement using visual tools* (2nd ed.). Thousand Oaks, CA: Corwin.

A review of research on thinking maps.

Jensen, E. (2005). *Teaching with the brain in mind.* Alexandria, VA: Association for Supervision and Curriculum Development.

A review of brain research.

Johnson, D., & Johnson, R. (2009). An educational psychology success story: Social interdependence and cooperative learning. *Educational Researcher, 38*(5), 365–379.

Research on cooperative learning.

Johnson, D., Johnson, R., & Roseth, C. (2010). Cooperative learning in middle schools: Interrelationships of relationship and achievement. *Middle Grades Research Journal* 5(1), 1–18.

A summary of research on cooperative learning.

Johnson, C., Zhang, D., & Kahle, J. (2012). Effective science instruction: Impact on high-stakes assessment performance. *Research in Middle Level Education, 35*(9), 1–14.

A longitudinal research study finding that students who experience inquiry-based science instruction outperformed other students.

Lengel, T., & Kuczala, M. (2010). *The kinesthetic classroom: Teaching and learning through movement.* Thousand Oaks, CA: Corwin and the Regional Training Center.

A summary of 17 action research projects related to movement in the classroom. The studies point to conclusions that using movement and other kinesthetic activities in the classroom can have the following benefits: preparation of students' brains and bodies for learning; increased student motivation; more positive learning states and classroom environments; increased test scores due to easier recall and retention of information; and increased student participation, attention, and engagement.

Marks, H. (2000). Student engagement in instructional activity: Patterns in the elementary, middle, and high school years. *American Educational Research Journal, 37*(1), 153–184.

A research study of 3,669 students representing 143 social studies and math classrooms that found reform initiatives substantially influenced student engagement.

Medina, J. (2014). *Brain rules: 12 principles for surviving and thriving at work, home, and school.* Seattle, WA: Pear Press.

A summary of brain research.

Merchie, E., & Van Keer, H. (2013). Schematizing and processing informational texts with mind maps in fifth and sixth grade. *Middle Grades Research Journal, 8*(3), 61–81.

A research study of fifth and sixth graders that found they were able to learn to process information texts using mind maps.

Musoleno, R. R., & White, G. P. (2010). Influences of high-stakes testing on middle school mission and practice. *Research in Middle Level Education, 34*(3), 1–10.

A survey of middle school educators examining the effects of high-stakes testing on middle school practices. Results show that since the implementation of the No Child Left Behind Act, developmentally appropriate practices in middle schools have been altered for the purpose of test preparation.

National Assessment of Educational Progress. (2007). *2006 U.S. History.* Retrieved from http://nces. ed.gov/nationsreportcard/ushistory/

Research data suggesting that when teachers use a variety of teaching approaches, students outperform their peers in traditional classrooms.

Nesin, G. (2012). Active learning. In *This we believe in action: Implementing successful middle level schools* (pp. 17–27). Westerville, OH: Association for Middle Level Education.

A literature review on active learning in the middle grades.

Oliveira, A., Wilcox, K., Angelis, J., Applebee, A., Amodeo, V., & Snyder, M. (2013). Best practice in middle-school science. *Journal of Science Teacher Education, 24,* 297–322.

A research study of seven middle schools that explore whether best practices correlate with higher student performance in science.

Slavin, R. (2011). Instruction based on cooperative learning. In R. E. Mayer & P. A. Alexander (Eds.), *Handbook of research on learning and instruction* (pp. 344–360). New York: Routledge.

A summary of research on cooperative learning.

Smart, J., & Marshall, J. (2013). Interactions between classroom discourse, teacher questioning, and student cognitive engagement in middle school science. *Journal of Science Teacher Education, 24,* 249–267.

A research study of ten middle school science classrooms. Findings include a positive correlation between classroom discourse and student cognitive level.

Spires, H., Lee, J., Turner, K., & Johnson, J. (2008). Having our say: Middle grade student perspectives on school, technologies, and academic engagement. *Journal of Research on Technology in Education, 40*(4), 497–515.

A research study of 4,000 middle grades students to examine the middle school student perspective on what they need to be engaged. The study found that the use of technology is important because it is a part of everyday life for students.

Swan, K., Vahey, P., van't Hooft, M., Kratcoski, A., Rafanan, K., Stanford, T., Yarnall, L., & Cook, D. (2013). Problem-based learning across the curriculum: Exploring the efficacy of a cross-curricular application of preparation for future learning. *Interdisciplinary Journal of Problem-Based Learning, 7*(1), 91–110.

A research study involving seventh grade students learning about data literacy. Findings indicate that problem-based learning supports the development of data literacy.

Thomas, J. (2000). *A review of research on project-based learning.* San Rafael, CA: The Autodesk Foundation. Retrieved from: http://www.bobpearlman.org/BestPractices/PBL_Research.pdf

A summary of research on project-based learning.

Tsay, M., & Brady, M. (2010). A case study of cooperative learning and communication pedagogy: Does working in teams make a difference? *Journal of the Scholarship of Teaching and Learning, 10*(2), 78–89.

A research study of active learning pedagogy. The study found that active participation in team-based learning had a positive relationship with academic performance.

Turner, J., Christensen, A., Kackar-Cam, H., Trucano, M., & Fulmer, S. (2014). Enhancing students' engagement: Report of a 3-year intervention with middle school teachers. *American Educational Research Journal, 51*(6), 1195–1226.

A study of 32 middle school teachers in one school examining improvement in student engagement.

Valentine, J., & Collins, J. (2001, April). *Student engagement and achievement on high-stakes tests: A HLM analysis across 68 middle schools.* Paper presented at the American Educational Research Association, Annual Conference, New Orleans, LA.

A study involving 10,000 classroom observations in middle schools over multiple years. Higher-order student engagement led to increases in standardized achievement

Walberg, H. (1999). Productive teaching. In H. C. Waxman & H. J. Walberg (Eds.), *New directions for teaching practice research* (pp. 75–104). Berkeley, CA: McCutchen.

Analysis of 93 research studies that found the use of games during instruction increased student achievement.

Whittingham, J., & Huffman, S. (2009). The effects of book clubs on the reading attitudes of middle school students. *Reading improvement, 46*(3), 130–136.

A study involving 60 middle school students in two schools. Findings indicate that book clubs have a positive effect on students who have a resistance to reading.

Yair, G. (2000). Not just about time: Instructional practices and productive time in school. *Educational Administration Quarterly, 36*(4), 485–512.

A research study of student engagement and instructional methods. The more active the instructional method, the higher the rates of student reports of engagement.

References

Allen, R. (2008). *Green light classrooms: Teaching techniques that accelerate learning.* Victoria, Australia: Hawker Brownlow.

Allinder, R. (1994). The relationships between efficacy and the instructional practices of special education teachers and consultants. *Teacher Education and Special Education, 17,* 86–95.

Anderson, L., & Krathwohl, D. (2001). *A taxonomy for learning, teaching, and assessing: A revision of Bloom's Taxonomy of educational objectives.* Boston: Pearson.

Anderson, R., Greene, M., & Loewen, P. (1988). Relationships among teachers' and students' thinking skills, sense of efficacy, and student achievement. *Alberta Journal of Educational Research, 34*(2), 148–165.

Angelo, T.A., & Cross, K. P. (1993). *Classroom assessment techniques: A handbook for college teachers* (2nd ed.). San Francisco, CA: Jossey-Bass.

Apple, M., & Beane, J. (2007). *Democratic schools: Lessons in powerful education* (2nd ed.). Portsmouth, NH: Heinemann.

Arendt, H. (1958). *The human condition.* Chicago: University of Chicago Press.

Aronson, E., Blaney, N., Stephin, C., Sikes, J., & Snapp, M. (1978). *The jigsaw classroom.* Beverly Hills, CA: Sage.

Astin, A. (1985). *Achieving educational excellence.* San Francisco: Jossey-Bass.

Baker, E., Pearson, P., & Rozendal, M. (2010). Theoretical perspectives and literacy studies: An exploration of roles and insight. In E. A. Baker (Ed.), *The new literacies: Multiple perspectives on research and practice* (pp. 1–22). New York: Guilford Press.

Bandura, A. (1986). *Social foundations of thought and action: A social cognitive theory.* Englewood Cliffs, NJ: Prentice-Hall.

Bandura, A. (1997). *Self-efficacy: The exercise of control.* New York: W. H. Freeman.

Bandura, A. (2001). Social cognitive theory: An agentic perspective. *Annual Review of Psychology, 52,* 1–26.

Bennett, C. (2014). Creating cultures of participation to promote mathematical discourse. *Middle School Journal, 46*(2), 20–25.

Bishop, P., & Downes, J. (2013). Technology in the middle grades classroom. In P. G. Andrews (Ed.), *Research to guide practice in middle grades education* (pp. 267–302). Westerville, OH: Association for Middle Level Education.

Bloor, E. (2006). *Tangerine.* Boston: Houghton Mifflin Harcourt.

Bonwell, C. & Eison, J. (1991). *Active learning: Creating excitement in the classroom.* (ASHE-ERIC Higher Education Report No. 1). Washington, DC: The George Washington University School of Education and Human Development.

Bransford, J., Brown, A., & Cocking, R. (2003). *How people learn: Brain, mind, experience, and school.* Washington, DC: National Academy Press.

Brighton, K. (2007). *Coming of age: The education and development of young adolescents.* Westerville, OH: National Middle School Association.

Brodhagen, B., & Gorud, S. (2012). Multiple learning approaches. In *This we believe in action: Implementing successful middle level schools* (pp. 47–61). Westerville, OH: Association for Middle Level Education.

Byrnes, J. (2001). *Cognitive development and learning in instructional contexts.* Boston: Allyn and Bacon.

Caine, R., Caine, G., McClintic, C., & Klimek, K. (2009). *12 brain/mind learning principles in action: Developing executive functions of the human brain* (2nd ed.). Thousand Oaks, CA: Corwin.

Caissy, G. (1994). *Early adolescence: Understanding the 10 to 15 year old.* Cambridge, MA: Perseus.

Cameron, S. (2004). *The reading activity handbook: Purposeful reading responses to enrich your literacy programme.* New Zealand: Pearson.

Campbell, K. (2014). Get your students moving: Incorporating movement in the classroom keeps students and their brains engaged in learning. *AMLE Magazine, 1*(7), 12–14.

Carbonneau, K., Marley, S., & Selig, J. (2013). A meta-analysis of the efficacy of teaching mathematics with concrete manipulatives. *Journal of Educational Psychology, 105*(2), 380–400.

Carrejo, D., & Reinhartz, J. (2014). Facilitating conceptual change through modeling in the middle school science classroom. *Middle School Journal, 46*(2), 10–17.

Casey, H. (2012). Multimodal learning clubs. *Middle School Journal, 44*(2), 39–48.

Castle, K. (2006). Autonomy through pedagogical research. *Teaching and Teacher Education, 22,* 1094–1103.

Collins, J., & O'Brien, N. (2003). *The Greenwood dictionary of education.* Westport, CT: Greenwood.

Cornelius-White, J., & Harbaugh, A. (2010). *Learner-centered instruction: Building relationships for student success.* Thousand Oaks, CA: Sage.

Cross, K. (1991). Every teacher a researcher, every classroom a laboratory. *Tribal College: A Journal of American Indian Higher Education, 2*(4), 7–12.

Danielewicz, J. (2001). *Teaching selves: Identity, pedagogy, and teacher education.* Albany, NY: State University of New York Press.

Day, J., Spiegel, D., McLellan, J., & Brown, V. (2002). *Moving forward with literature circles: How to plan, manage, and evaluate literature circles that deepen understanding and foster a love of reading.* New York: Scholastic.

Debbink, K. (2008). Who would you help? In R. Stone (Ed.), *Best practices for teaching social studies: What award-winning classroom teachers do* (pp. 35–36). Thousand Oaks, CA: Corwin Press.

Dewey, J. (1897). My pedagogic creed. *School Journal, 54,* 77–80.

Dewey, J. (1924). *Democracy in education.* New York: Macmillan.

Dewey, J. (1931). *The way out of educational confusion.* Westport, CT: Greenwood Press.

Dewey, J. (1933). *How we think.* Chicago: Henry Regnery.

DiCamillo, L., & Gradwell, J. (2012). Using simulations to teach middle grades U.S. history in an age of accountability. *Research in Middle Level Education, 35*(7), 1–16.

Dixon, E. (2013). *Helping boys learn: 6 secrets for teaching boys in the classroom.* Toronto: Create Space.

Downes, J., & Bishop, P. (2012). Educators engage digital natives and learn from their experiences with technology. *Middle School Journal, 43*(5), 6–15.

Dreon, O., Kerper, R., & Landis, J. (2011). Digital storytelling: A tool for teaching and learning in the YouTube generation. *Middle School Journal, 42*(5), 4–9.

Duckworth, A., Quinn, P., & Seligman, M. (2009). Positive predictors of teacher effectiveness. *The Journal of Positive Psychology, 4*(6), 540–547.

Duffy, G. (2002). Visioning and the development of outstanding teachers. *Reading Research and Instruction. 41*(4), 331–334.

Duffy, G., & Hoffman, J. (1999). In pursuit of an illusion: The flawed search for a perfect method. *Reading Teacher, 53*, 10–17.

Edwards, S. (2011). Managing a standards-based classroom: A specially designed professional development program supports quality instruction by novice teachers. *Mathematics in the Middle School, 17*(5), 282–286.

Edwards, S. (2014). *Getting them to talk: A guide to leading discussions in middle grades classrooms.* Westerville, OH: Association for Middle Level Education.

Edwards, S. (2015). Active learning in the middle grades classroom: Overcoming the barriers to implementation. *Middle Grades Research Journal, 10*(1), 65–81.

Edwards, S., Kemp, A., & Page, C. (2014). The middle school philosophy: Do we practice what we preach or do we preach something different? *Current Issues in Middle Level Education, 19*(1), 13–19.

Epstein, A. (2007). *The intentional teacher.* Washington, DC: National Association for the Education of Young Children.

Faber, S. (2006). *How to teach reading when you're not a reading teacher.* Nashville, TN: Incentive Publications.

Feinstein, S. (2009). *Secrets of the teenage brain: Research-based strategies for reaching and teaching today's adolescents* (2nd ed.). Thousand Oaks, CA: Corwin.

Finders, M., & Hynds, S. (2007). *Language arts and literacy in the middle grades: Planning, teaching, and assessing learning.* Upper Saddle River, NJ: Pearson.

Findley, N. (2005). What do we mean by limited attention span? *Phi Delta Kappan, 86*(9), 652–653.

Fisher, D., Brozo, W., Frey, N., & Ivey, G. (2011). *50 instructional routines to develop content literacy.* Boston: Pearson.

Fogarty, R. (2009). *Brain-compatible classrooms* (3rd ed.). Victoria, Australia: Hawker Brownlow.

Frayer, D., Frederick, W., & Klausmeier, H. (1969). *A schema for testing the level of concept mastery* (Technical Report #16). Madison, WI: Wisconsin Center for Education Research.

Fredrickson, R., Dunlap, K., & McMahan, S. (2013). Cooperative learning theory. In B. Irby, G. Brown, R. Lara-Alecio, & S. Jackson (Eds.), *The handbook of educational theories* (pp. 199–210). Charlotte, NC: Information Age.

Fredrickson, R., McMahan, S., & Dunlap, K. (2013). Problem-based learning theory. In B. Irby, G. Brown, R. Lara-Alecio, & S. Jackson (Eds.), *The handbook of educational theories* (pp. 199–210). Charlotte, NC: Information Age.

Freire, P. (2001). *Pedagogy of the oppressed: 30th anniversary edition.* New York: Continuum International.

Friend, M., & Bursuck, W. (2012). *Including students with special needs: A practical guide for classroom teachers.* (6th ed.). Boston, MA: Pearson.

Greene, M. (1978). *Landscapes of learning.* New York: Teachers College Press.

Gregory, G., & Herndon, L. (2010). *Differentiated instructional strategies for the block schedule.* Thousand Oaks, CA: Corwin.

Guskey, T. (1988). Teacher efficacy, self-concept, and attitudes toward the implementation of instructional innovation. *Teaching and Teacher Education, 4,* 63–69.

Hagevik, R. (2011). Fostering 21st century learning with geospatial technologies. *Middle School Journal, 43*(1), 16–23.

Hallman, R. (1967). Techniques for creative teaching. *Journal for Creative Behavior, 1* (3), 325-330.

Hammerness, K. (2001). Teachers' visions: The role of personal ideals in school reform. *Journal of Educational Change, 2,* 143–163.

Hansen, R., & Hansen, K. (2010). What do employers really want? Top skills and values employers seek from job-seekers. *Quintessential Careers.* Retrieved from http://www.quintcareers.com/job_skills_values.html

Harmin, M. (1995). *Inspiring active learning: Strategies of instruction.* White Plains, NY: Inspiring Strategy Institute.

Harris, B. (2011). *Battling boredom: 99 strategies to spark student engagement.* Larchmont, NY: Eye on Education.

Hearn, M., & Winner, M. (2013). *Teach math with the Wii: Engage your K–7 students through gaming technology.* Eugene, OR: International Society for Technology in Education.

Hernandez-Ramos, P., & De La Paz, S. (2009). Learning history in middle school by designing multimedia in a project-based learning experience. *Journal of Research on Technology in Education, 42*(2), 151–173.

Herr, N. (2008). *The sourcebook for teaching science: Strategies, activities, and instructional resources.* San Francisco, CA: Jossey-Bass.

Igel, C. & Urquhart, V. (2012). Generation z, meet cooperative learning. *Middle School Journal, 43*(4), 16-21.

International Society for Technology in Education. (2015). *ISTE standards for students.* Retrieved from: http://www.iste.org/standards/iste-standards/standards-for-students

Jensen, E. (2005). *Teaching with the brain in mind* (2nd ed.). Alexandria, VA: Association for Supervision and Curriculum Development.

Jensen, R. (2008). *Catalyst teaching: High-impact teaching techniques for the science classroom.* Victoria, Australia: Hawker Brownlow.

Jewitt, C., & Kress, G. (2003). *Multimodal literacy.* New York: Peter Lang.

Kagan, S. (2001). Kagan structures for emotional intelligence. *Kagan Online Magazine, 4*(4).

Kagan, S., & Kagan, M. (2009). *Kagan cooperative learning.* San Clemente, CA: Kagan.

Kaplan, S., & Cannon, M. (2001). *Curriculum starter cards: Developing differentiated lessons for gifted students.* Waco, TX: Prufrock Press.

Karchmer-Klein, R. (2013). Best practices in using technology to support writing. In S. Graham, C. MacArthur, & J. Fitzgerald (Eds.), *Best practices in writing instruction* (2nd Ed.) (pp. 309–331). New York: Guilford Press.

Keeley, P. (2008). *Science formative assessment: 75 practical strategies for linking assessment, instruction, and learning.* Thousand Oaks, CA; Arlington, VA: Corwin & National Science Teachers Association.

Kellough, R. & Kellough, N. (1978). *A resource guide for secondary school teaching,* (2nd ed). Upper Saddle River, NJ: Prentice Hall

Kellough, R., & Kellough, N. (2008). *Teaching young adolescents: Methods and resources for middle grades teaching* (5th ed.). Upper Saddle River, NJ: Pearson Merrill Prentice Hall.

Kilbane, C., & Milman, N. (2014). *Teaching models: Designing instruction for 21st century learners.* Upper Saddle River, NJ: Pearson.

Lattimer, H., & Riordan, R. (2011). Project-based learning engages students in meaningful work. *Middle School Journal, 43*(2), 18–23.

Lengel, T., & Kuczala, M. (2010). *The kinesthetic classroom: Teaching and learning through movement.* Thousand Oaks, CA; West Randolph, NJ: Corwin and the Regional Training Center.

Macauley, J. (2014). *Kick me: Making vocabulary interactive.* Retrieved from: https://www.teachingchannel.org/videos/making-vocabulary-lesson-interactive

Maddux, C., Johnson, D., & Willis, J. (2001). *Educational computing: Learning with tomorrow's technologies.* Needham Heights, MA: Allyn & Bacon.

Martinez, S., & Stager, G. (2013). *Invent to learn: Making, tinkering, and engineering in the classroom.* Torrance, CA: Constructing Modern Knowledge Press.

Marzano, R. (2010). The art and science of teaching: Using games to enhance student achievement. *Educational Leadership, 67*(5), 71–72.

McEwin, C., & Greene, M. (2010). Results and recommendations from the 2009 national surveys of randomly selected and highly successful middle level schools. *Middle School Journal, 42*(1), 49–63.

Medina, J. (2014). *Brain rules: 12 principles for surviving and thriving at work, home, and school.* Seattle, WA: Pear Press.

Melber, L., & Hunter, A. (2010). *Integrating language arts and social studies: 25 strategies for K–8 inquiry-based learning.* Thousand Oaks, CA: Sage.

Merchie, E., & Van Keer, H. (2013). Schematizing and processing informational texts with mind maps in fifth and sixth grades. *Middle Grades Research Journal, 8*(3), 61–81.

Meyers, C., & Jones, T. (1993). *Promoting active learning: Strategies for the college classroom.* San Francisco, CA: Jossey-Bass.

Michael, J. (2006). Where's the evidence that active learning works? *Advances in Physiology Education, 30,* 159–167. doi: 10.1152/advan.00053.2006

Moore, K. (2009). *Effective instructional strategies: From theory to practice* (2nd ed). Los Angeles: Sage.

Moore, W., & Esselman, M. (1992, April). *Teacher efficacy, power, school climate and achievement: A desegregating district's experience.* Paper presented at the annual meeting of the American Educational Research Association, San Francisco.

Musoleno, R., & White, G. (2010). Influences of high-stakes testing on middle school mission and practice. *Research in Middle Level Education Online, 34*(3).

Narayan, R., Rodriguez, C., Araujo, J., Shaqlaih, A., & Moss, G. (2013). Constructivism-constructivist learning theory. In B. Irby, G. Brown, R. Lara-Alecio, & S. Jackson (Eds.), *The handbook of educational theories* (pp. 169–183). Charlotte, NC: Information Age.

National Council of Teachers of English. (2015). *Adolescent literacy: A policy research brief.* Retrieved from http://www.ncte.org/positions/instruction

National Council of Teachers of Mathematics. (1991). *Professional standards for teaching mathematics.* Reston, VA: National Council of Teachers of Mathematics.

National Council of Teachers of Mathematics. (2000). *Principles and standards for school mathematics.* Reston, VA: National Council of Teachers of Mathematics.

National Council of Teachers of Mathematics. (2014). *Principles to actions: Ensuring mathematical success for all.* Reston, VA: National Council of Teachers of Mathematics.

National Council for the Social Studies (2010). National curriculum standards for social studies: *A framework for teaching, learning and assessment.* Retrieved from http://www.socialstudies.org/standards

National Governors Association Center for Best Practices and Council of Chief State School Officers. (2015). *Common core state standards for mathematics: Standards for mathematical practice.* Retrieved from http://www.corestandards.org/Math/Practice/

National Middle School Association. (2010). *This we believe: Keys to educating young adolescents.* Westerville, OH: National Middle School Association.

National Science Teachers Association. (2015a). *NSTA position statement.* Retrieved from: http://www.nsta.org/about/positions/natureofscience.aspx

National Science Teachers Association. (2015b). *Science and engineering practices.* Retrieved from: http://ngss.nsta.org/ PracticesFull.aspx

Nesin, G. (2012). Active learning. In *This we believe in action: Implementing successful middle level schools* (pp. 17–27). Westerville, OH: Association for Middle Level Education.

Neufeld, V., & Barrows, H. (1974). The Mcmaster philosophy: An approach to medical education. *Journal of Medical Education, 49*(11), 1040–1050.

Noe, K., & Johnson, N. (1999). *Getting started with literature circles.* Norwood, MA: Christopher-Gordon Publishers.

Novak, J., & Gowin, D. (1996). *Learning how to learn.* New York: Cambridge University Press.

Oakeshott, M., & Fuller, T. (2001). *The voice of liberal learning: Michael Oakeshott on education.* New Haven, CT: Yale University Press.

Ohler, J. (2008). *Digital storytelling in the classroom: New media pathways to literacy, learning, and creativity.* Thousand Oaks, CA: Corwin Press.

Omundson, J. (2014). Cardboard boat building in math class. *Middle School Journal, 46*(2), 3-9.

Parsons, S. C., Mokhtari, K., Yellin, D., & Orwig, R. (2011). Literature study groups: Literacy learning "with legs". *Middle School Journal, 42*(5), 22–30.

Partnership for 21st Century Skills. (2006). *Results that matter: 21st Century skills and high school reform.* Tucson, AZ: Author.

Pate, P. E. (2013). Academically excellent curriculum, instruction, and assessment. In P. G. Andrews (Ed.), *Research to guide practice in middle grades education.* (pp. 165–186). Westerville, OH: Association for Middle Level Education.

Petress, K. (2008). What is meant by active learning? *Education, 128*(4), 566–569.

Piaget, J. (1972). *To understand is to invent*. New York: The Viking Press.

Piccolo, D., Harbaugh, A., Carter, T., Capraro, M., & Capraro, R. (2008). Quality of instruction: Examining discourse in middle school mathematics instruction. *Journal of Advanced Academics, 19*, 376–410.

Prensky, M. (2001). Digital natives, digital immigrants. *On the horizon, 9*(5).

Putnam, V., & Paulus, P. (2009). Brainstorming, brainstorming rules and decision making. *The Journal of Creative Behavior, 43*(1), 23–39.

Putnam, E., & Rommel-Esham, K. (2004). Using oral history to study change: An integrated approach. *The Social Studies, 95*(5), 201–205.

Rideout, V., Foehr, U., & Roberts, D. (2010). *Generation M2: Media in the lives of 8- to 18-year-olds*. Menlo Park, CA: Henry J. Kaiser Family Foundation. Retrieved from http://www.kff.org/entmedai/mh012010pkg.cfm

Ross, J. (1992). Teacher efficacy and the effect of coaching on student achievement. *Canadian Journal of Education, 17*(1), 51–65.

Runde, J. (2013, May 17). Five for Friday—Test prep and angry birds [Web log post]. Retrieved from http://www.rundesroom.com/2013/05/five-for-friday-test-prep-and-angry.html

Ruhl, K., Hughes, C., & Schloss, P. (1987). Using the pause procedure to enhance lecture recall. *Teacher Education and Special Education, 10*, 14–18.

Scales, P. (2010). Characteristics of young adolescents. In *This we believe: Keys to educating young adolescents* (pp. 63–62). Westerville, OH: National Middle School Association.

Schmidt, L. (2007). *Social studies that sticks: How to bring content and concepts to life.* Portsmouth, NH: Heinemann.

Schon, D. (1987). *Educating the reflective practitioner: Toward a design for teaching and learning in the profession.* San Francisco: Jossey-Bass.

Shulman, L., & Shulman, J. (2004). How and what teachers learn: A shifting perspective. *Journal of Curriculum Studies, 36,* 257–271.

Silver, D., Berckemeyer, J., & Baenen, J. (2015). *Deliberate optimism: Reclaiming the joy in education.* Thousand Oaks, CA: Corwin Press.

Sirinterlikci, A., Zane, L., & Sirinterlikci, A. (2009). Active learning through toy design and development. *Journal of Technology Studies, 35*(2), 14–22.

Spencer, J. (2008). *Everyone's invited: Interactive strategies that engage young adolescents.* Westerville, OH: National Middle School Association.

Spires, H., Hervey, L., Morris, G., & Stelpflug, C. (2012). Energizing project-based inquiry: Middle-grade students read, write, and create videos. *Journal of Adolescent & Adult Literacy 55*(6), 483–493.

Spires, H., Lee, J., Turner, K., & Johnson, J. (2008) Having our say: Middle grade student perspectives on school, technologies, and academic engagement. *Journal of Research on Technology in Education, 40*(4), 497–515.

Sprenger, M. (2007). *Memory 101 for educators.* Thousand Oaks, CA: Corwin.

Stein, M., Smith, M., Henningson, M., & Silver, E. (2009). *Implementing standards–based mathematics instruction: A casebook for professional development,* (2nd ed.). New York: Teachers College Press.

Stein, M., & Wang, M. (1988). Teacher development and school improvement: The process of teacher change. *Teaching and Teacher Education, 4,* 171–187.

Taranto, G., Dalbon, M., & Gaetano, J. (2011). Academic social networking brings web 2.0 technologies to the middle grades. *Middle School Journal, 42*(5), 12–19.

Tate, M. (2012). *Social studies worksheets don't grow dendrites: 20 instructional strategies that engage the brain.* Thousand Oaks, CA: Corwin.

Tate, M., & Phillips, W. (2011). *Science worksheets don't grow dendrites: 20 instructional strategies that engage the brain.* New York: Skyhorse.

Tiberius, R. (1986). Metaphors underlying the improvement of teaching and learning. *British Journal of Educational Technology, 17*(2), 144–156.

Tovani, C. (2004). *Do I really have to teach reading? Content comprehension, grades 6–12.* Portland, ME: Stenhouse.

Tschannen-Moran, M., & Hoy, A. (2001). Teacher efficacy: Capturing an elusive construct. *Teaching and Teacher Education, 17*(7), 783–805.

Udvari-Solner, A., & Kluth, P. (2008). *Joyful learning: Active and collaborative learning in inclusive classrooms.* Thousand Oaks, CA: Sage.

Vanides, J., Yin, Y., Tomita, M., & Ruiz-Primo, M. (2005). Using concept maps in the science classroom. *Science Scope, 28*(8), 27–31.

Van Scotter, R., White, W., Hartoonian, H., & Davis, J. (2007). A gateway to social studies through topical history. *Social Studies, 98*(6), 231–235.

Vaughn, M. (2013). Examining teacher agency: Why did Les leave the building? *The New Educator, 9*(2), 119–134.

Vaughn, M., & Faircloth, B. (2011). Understanding teacher visioning and agency during literacy instruction. In P. Dunston & L. Gambrell (Eds.), *60th yearbook of the Literacy Research Association* (pp. 156–164). Oak Creek, WI: Literacy Research Association.

Venn, J. (1880). On the diagrammatic and mechanical representation of propositions and reasonings. *Philosophical Magazine and Journal of Science.*

Vygotsky, L. (1962). *Thought and language.* Cambridge, MA: MIT Press.

Wagner, T. (2012). *Creating innovators: The making of young people who will change the world.* New York: Scribner.

Walsh, D. (2004). *Why do they act that way?* New York: Free Press.

Whittingham, J., & Huffman, S. (2009). The effects of book clubs on the reading attitudes of middle school students. *Reading improvement, 46*(3), 130–136.

Wilson, C. (2009). Planning and implementing inquiry-oriented activities for middle grades science. *Middle School Journal, 41*(2), 41–49.

Wood, G. (2004). A view from the field: NCLB's effects on classrooms and schools. In D. Meier & G. Wood (Eds.), *Many children left behind: How the No Child Left Behind Act is damaging our children and our schools* (pp. 33–50). Boston, MA: Beacon Press.

Zeichner, K., & Liston, D. (1996). *Reflective teaching: An introduction.* Mahwah, NJ: Lawrence Erlbaum Associates.

Zimmerman, M. (1995). Psychological empowerment: Issues and illustrations. *American Journal of Community Psychology, 23,* 581–599.

CPSIA information can be obtained
at www.ICGtesting.com
Printed in the USA
LVHW022327010921
696617LV00005B/10